WITHDRAWN

HARVARD LIBRARY

WITHDRAWN

The Role of God in Spinoza's Metaphysics

Also available from Continuum:

Aquinas and the Ship of Theseus, by Christopher Brown

The Demands of Taste in Kant's Aesthetics, by Brent Kalar

Descartes and the Metaphysics of Human Nature, by Justin Skirry

Dialectic of Romanticism, by David Roberts and Peter Murphy

Kierkegaard's Analysis of Radical Evil, by David A. Roberts

Leibniz Reinterpreted: The Harmony of Things, by Lloyd Strickland

Nietzsche and the Greeks, by Dale Wilkerson

The Philosophy of Miracles, by David Corner

Platonism, Music and the Listener's Share, by Christopher Norris

Popper's Theory of Science, by Carlos Garcia

Rousseau's Theory of Freedom, by Matthew Simpson

St. Augustine and the Theory of Just War, by John M. Mattox

St. Augustine of Hippo, by R. W. Dyson

Tolerance and the Ethical Life, by Andrew Fiala

Wittgenstein's Religious Point of View, by Tim Labron

The Role of God in Spinoza's Metaphysics

Sherry Deveaux

continuum

CONTINUUM International Publishing Group
The Tower Building
11 York Road
London SE1 7NX

80 Maiden Lane
Suite 704
New York
NY 10038

© Sherry Deveaux 2007

All rights reserved. No part of this publication may be reproduced or transmitted in any form or by any means, electronic or mechanical, including photocopying, recording, or any information storage or retrieval system, without prior permission in writing from the publishers.

British Library Cataloguing-in-Publication Data
A catalogue record for this book is available from the British Library.

ISBN: 0-8264-8888-9 (hardback)
9780826488886

Library of Congress Cataloging-in-Publication Data
A catalog record for this book is available from the Library of Congress.

Typeset by Servis Filmsetting Ltd, Manchester
Printed and bound in Great Britain by
Biddles Ltd, King's Lynn, Norfolk

B
3994
.D48
2007

Contents

INTRODUCTION	1
CHAPTER 1: THREE PROBLEMS	4
PROBLEM ONE : THE RELATION OF GOD TO THE ATTRIBUTES	4
PROBLEM TWO: THE ESSENCE OF GOD	7
PROBLEM THREE: THE TRUE CONCEPTION OF GOD	9
CHAPTER 2: THE "GOD IS THE THING THAT HAS ATTRIBUTES AND MODES AS PROPERTIES" INTERPRETATION	11
JONATHAN BENNETT'S INTERPRETATION	11
BENNETT AND THE THREE PROBLEMS	14
Discussion	15
CHAPTER 3: THE "GOD IS THE COLLECTION OF ATTRIBUTES" INTERPRETATION	19
EDWIN CURLEY'S INTERPRETATION	19
CURLEY AND THE THREE PROBLEMS	20
Discussion	21
AN ESSENCE VS THE ESSENCE OF GOD	25
ALAN DONAGAN'S INTERPRETATION	28
DONAGAN AND THE THREE PROBLEMS	29
Discussion	30
CHAPTER 4: THE "GOD IS THE TOTALITY OF ATTRIBUTES" INTERPRETATION	35
H. F. HALLETT'S INTERPRETATION	35
HALLETT AND THE THREE PROBLEMS	36
Discussion	37

THE STATUS OF THE ATTRIBUTES	39
STEVEN PARCHMENT'S INTERPRETATION	40
DESCARTES' THEORY OF DISTINCTION	42
PARCHMENT AND THE THREE PROBLEMS	43
The three problems and interpretive option one	45
Critique of interpretive option one	46
The three problems and interpretive option two	48
Critique of interpretive option two	48
The totality as homogenized	52

CHAPTER 5: BENEFITS AND DISADVANTAGES OF THE THREE INTERPRETATIONS — 54

BENEFITS AND DISADVANTAGES OF THE "GOD IS THE THING THAT HAS ATTRIBUTES AND MODES AS PROPERTIES" INTERPRETATION	54
BENEFITS AND DISADVANTAGES OF THE "GOD IS THE COLLECTION OF ATTRIBUTES" INTERPRETATION	55
BENEFITS AND DISADVANTAGES OF THE "GOD IS THE TOTALITY OF ATTRIBUTES" INTERPRETATION	59

CHAPTER 6: ESSENCES AND TRUE IDEAS IN SPINOZA — 62

ESSENCE AND 2d2	63
"TO PERTAIN TO", "TO CONSTITUTE", AND "TO EXPRESS" THE ESSENCE OF A THING	64
THE ESSENCE OF A THING	71
THE RELATIONSHIP BETWEEN A THING AND ITS ESSENCE	75
THE RELATIONSHIP BETWEEN A THING'S ESSENCE AND ITS POWER	77
THE NUMBER OF ATTRIBUTES	78
ADEQUATE AND TRUE IDEAS	81
DE DICTO/DE RE CONCEPTIONS	86
SUMMARY AND FURTHER CONSIDERATIONS	87

CHAPTER 7: THE ESSENCE OF SPINOZA'S GOD — 91

THE ESSENCE OF GOD AND 2d2	94
GOD AND DE DICTO/DE RE CONCEPTIONS	100
THE ESSENCE OF GOD	103

GOD	104
SOLUTIONS TO THE THREE PROBLEMS	105
Problem one: the relation of God to the attributes	105
Problem two: the essence of God	106
Problem three: the true conception of God	108
GOD AND THE ATTRIBUTES	111
THE DEFINITION OF GOD	112
THE DE RE IDEA OF GOD	118
NOTES	120
SELECT BIBLIOGRAPHY	138
INDEX	139

Introduction

Spinoza's theory of reality has both delighted and frustrated philosophers, both during his lifetime and since his death. Spinoza creates a tapestry of the universe and weaves into its fabric absolutely everything possible, for his reality is *absolutely* infinite and eternal. Indeed, Spinoza views reality as absolute perfection. While he strains to incorporate all being into his theory, his philosophy, according to some, suffers from the stress. Spinoza's concept of God, the primary concept of his most notable work, the *Ethics*, has fueled continual and heated controversy among Spinoza scholars.

Although there are many interpretations of Spinoza's God, most philosophers would agree with the thesis that, for Spinoza, reality consists of nothing other than God, the attributes, and modes. Spinoza's concept of the attributes of God, on the other hand, is hard to understand. The attributes of God have consequently been a subject of intense debate, and have borne the brunt of countless odd and dismissive interpretations. Although some may claim that the position of the attributes in Spinoza's theory of reality can easily be clarified, numerous other interpretations make it clear that his concept of the attributes can cause profound and manifold problems for any philosopher who takes Spinoza's use of the term seriously.

I will approach the topic of the attributes and their place in Spinoza's theory of reality by dealing with the problems that arise whenever the attributes of God are studied and discussed. In Chapter 1, I will set up the three main problems that arise regarding God and the attributes in Spinoza's metaphysics. They are: (1) the problem of the relation of God to the attributes, (2) the problem of the essence of God, and (3) the problem of the true conception of God. The purpose of this work is to seek satisfactory solutions to these problems. In order to do so, it will be necessary to consider the views of contemporary Spinoza scholars on the subject of God and the attributes.

In Chapters 2, 3, and 4, I will examine three interpretations of God and the attributes in Spinoza: respectively, that of Jonathan Bennett, according to which God is the thing that has the attributes and modes as properties, that of Edwin Curley and Alan Donagan, according to which God is the collection of attributes, and that of H. F. Hallett and Steven Parchment, according to which God is the totality of attributes. After providing a succinct overview of each philosopher's stance on God and the attributes in Spinoza, I will examine each of these views relative to the three problems laid out in Chapter 1. I will then evaluate each philosopher's interpretation. My goal is to demonstrate which of the problems each commentator can successfully address in his interpretation of God and the attributes.[1] In Chapter 5, I will review the strengths and weaknesses of each interpretation.

After reviewing and evaluating contemporary interpretations of God and the attributes in Spinoza I will move on to other important topics. In Chapter 6, I will discuss topics in Spinoza that need to be understood before we can go on to discover the correct solutions to the three problems. I will deal with Spinoza's concept of the essence of a thing; in particular, I will consider what it means for something to pertain to, to constitute, to express, and just to be the essence of a thing. This process will naturally include a treatment of 2d2—Spinoza's purported definition of the essence of a thing.[2] Further, I will inquire into the nature of the relationship between a thing and its essence, and into the relationship between a thing's essence and its power. Once we have a clearer understanding of the essences of things in Spinoza's metaphysics, I will review the nature of adequate ideas for Spinoza, and the relation of adequacy to truth. In addition, I will discuss the difference between de dicto and de re conceptions of things, showing that there are both de dicto and de re conceptions relative to God. In this chapter I will also consider whether the attributes are finite or infinite in number.

Finally, in Chapter 7, I will suggest an interpretation of God and the attributes that is motivated by Spinoza's claim in 1p34 that God's power is God's essence. One of the main benefits of this interpretation is that it avoids the problem of the divisibility of God while simultaneously offering a comprehensible view of Spinoza's God.[3] I will claim that an adequate idea of the essence of God is a de re conception of God, and I will invoke Michael Della Rocca's account of the opacity of attribute contexts in order to support my view of de re conceptions of God. I will explain what the attributes *are* for Spinoza and the *role* that attributes play in his understanding of reality. I will show that by viewing the attributes through this alternative interpretation many of the problems incurred by other interpretations can be solved or avoided altogether. Indeed, I will resolve the three problems posed in Chapter 1.

In my interpretation of God and the attributes I will concur with Steven Parchment's initial approach to the problem. That is, I agree with Parchment's emphasis on 2d2 in his consideration of the relation between God and the attributes.[4] I will show that clearly understanding Spinoza's meaning in 2d2 (and therefore understanding what the essence of God is) leads to a plausible interpretation of the attributes of God. Also, I will show that the most useful aspect of Hallett's view is not his interpretation of the attributes as indiscerptible in God (a view that Parchment seems to espouse), but rather his emphasis on Spinoza's God as the maximally active entity. I will then go on to discuss Spinoza's claim that the essence of a thing is given by the definition of the thing (i.e. the definition of the thing is the statement of the essence of the thing). I will then consider the definition of Spinoza's God (1d6) and question whether that definition correlates with his claim in 1p34 that God's power is God's essence.[5] I will argue that God's essence is absolutely infinite and eternal power, and that power is what is constituted and expressed by each of the infinite attributes.

Chapter 1

Three Problems

Problem one: the relation of God to the attributes

I will address three main problems regarding God and the attributes. First, what is the relation of God to the attributes? Currently, there seems to be a general consensus among Spinoza scholars regarding the relation between God and the attributes. A review of contemporary literature on Spinoza's metaphysics reveals an overwhelming tendency to view God as somehow identical with the attributes. The nature of that identity, however, varies among commentators. Some claim that God is the collection of attributes—that is, the sum of the discrete attributes—while others hold the view that God is the totality of attributes—that is, a whole consisting of non-discrete attributes.

These interpretations of God and the attributes in Spinoza's metaphysics are motivated in part by statements that, on the surface, appear to support the view that God and the attributes are identical. Consider 1p4 and its demonstration:

> 1p4: Two or more distinct things are distinguished from one another, either by a difference in the attributes of the substances or by a difference in their affections.

> 1p4d: Whatever is, is either in itself or in another (by A1), i.e. (by D3 and D5), outside the intellect there is nothing except substances and their affections. Therefore, there is nothing outside the intellect through which a number of things can be distinguished from one another except substances, *or* what is the same (by D4), their attributes, and their affections, q.e.d.

Others point to Spinoza's bold claim in the demonstration of 1p15 as support for the view that God is identical with the attributes:

> 1p15d: Except for God, there neither is, nor can be conceived, any substance (by P14), i.e. (by D3), thing that is in itself and is conceived through itself. But modes (by D5) can neither be nor be conceived without substance. So they can be in the divine nature alone, and can be conceived through it alone. But except for substances and modes there is nothing (by A1). Therefore, [NS: everything is in God and] nothing can be or be conceived without God, q.e.d.

Given this statement, one might claim that the attributes must be either substances or modes. Since the attributes are not modes, they must be substances (i.e. the attributes must be God). If God is not identical with the attributes, then any other interpretation must be able to account for claims like those in the demonstrations of 1p4 and 1p15.[1]

Although interpretations of God as identical with the attributes may seem straightforward enough, they can pose problems for other interpretations of Spinoza's views. For example, some commentators hold a subjectivist view regarding the attributes and have suggested that the attributes have no reality outside the intellect. On this reading the attributes are a function of the intellect but do not, in themselves, exist as real entities. Spinoza's definition of the term "attribute" is 1d4:

> By attribute I understand what the intellect perceives of a substance, as constituting its essence.

Some commentators who hold the subjectivist view claim that it is questionable, at the very least, whether the attributes do constitute the essence of God, since the attributes are "what the intellect perceives as" constituting the essence of a substance. Subjectivists frequently claim that the intellect merely *perceives* the attributes as constituting the essence of God. In other words, on this view, the intellect is mistaken. If the subjectivist view is correct and the attributes have no existence outside the intellect, then the stance that God is identical with the attributes becomes obscure and abstruse. Whether the attributes are subjective or objective in nature, then, is an issue that must be probed and answered. God and the attributes can be identical entities only if the attributes exist as more than ideas in the intellect.

Other commentators interpret the attributes as objective in nature, that is, having existence outside the intellect. Indeed, some commentators claim both that the attributes constitute the essence of God, and that the attributes are somehow identical with God. There are problems with this objectivist view. What constitutes the essence of a thing might not be identical with the thing, since things might not be identical with their essences. Hence, it follows that what constitutes the essence of God might not be identical with God. One can therefore draw the conclusion that Spinoza's definition of attribute does not commit him to the claim that God is identical with one or all of the attributes.

Questions regarding the number of attributes also naturally arise at this point. By 2p1 and 2p2 we know that there are at least two attributes of God:

2p1: Thought is an attribute of God, or God is a thinking thing.

2p2: Extension is an attribute of God, or God is an extended thing.

According to 1d6, God is an absolutely infinite being.[2] Given 1p9, then, one might think that God has more than two attributes:

1p9: The more reality or being each thing has, the more attributes belong to it.

It has been suggested that since God has infinite reality the quantity of attributes must also be infinite. Are thought and extension the only attributes, or is there an infinity of attributes? How does the number of attributes affect interpretations of God and the attributes in Spinoza's metaphysics? Spinoza refers at times to the possibility of other attributes, though he concedes that he cannot know any attributes other than thought and extension.[3] I will discuss the question of the number of attributes in Spinoza's metaphysics and entertain various stances on the subject. It may turn out that the number of attributes does not pose a problem for Spinoza. If that is the case, then that may also be the reason why Spinoza entertained the possibility of the existence of more than two attributes without showing much concern for the consequences of that view. I will consider this possibility in my interpretation of the relation between God and the attributes in Spinoza's metaphysics.

Problem two: the essence of God

What is the essence of God? Commentators frequently suggest that the attributes are the essence of God. In evaluating this opinion one must consider an important definition in Spinoza's metaphysics—2d2:

> I say that to the essence of any thing belongs that which, being given, the thing is [NS: also] necessarily posited and which, being taken away, the thing is necessarily [NS: also] taken away; or that without which the thing can neither be nor be conceived, and which can neither be nor be conceived without the thing.

If the attributes satisfy this definition relative to God, then the attributes are that without which God can neither be nor be conceived and, vice versa, the attributes can neither be nor be conceived without God. In other words, neither God nor the attributes can be or be conceived without the other. The appropriate question to ask, of course, is whether it is one attribute, the collection of attributes, or the totality of attributes which satisfies 2d2. If, on the other hand, the attributes are not the essence of God, then the appropriate question to ask is: what satisfies the stipulations of 2d2 relative to God?

Although many commentators accept 2d2 as Spinoza's definition of the term "essence", others question this assumption. Donagan, for example, thinks that 2d2 is the definition of "what pertains to the essence of a thing". This interpretation of 2d2 may have important ramifications. I will consider this view in my treatment of the essence of God.

A critical examination of Spinoza's concept of attribute, then, will necessarily require a clear understanding of Spinoza's concept of essence. Specifically, a clear understanding of the essence of Spinoza's God will be required. In addition to a thorough exposition of 2d2, an understanding of the essence of God will require an evaluation of Spinoza's claim in 1p34 that God's power is God's essence. A thorough investigation of the attributes of God, therefore, will necessarily involve a careful analysis of how Spinoza understands God, attribute, essence, and power.

Whether the attributes *are* the essence of God or not, it seems clear enough that, for Spinoza, the attributes both constitute and express the essence of God. Spinoza's first mention of the attributes constituting the essence of God is found in 1d4, which says that the intellect perceives the attributes as constituting the essence of substance; and the first mention of the attributes expressing the essence of God is in 1d6:

> By God I understand a being absolutely infinite, i.e., a substance consisting of an infinity of attributes, of which each one expresses an eternal and infinite essence.

What does it mean for the attributes to constitute and express the essence of God? Does "constitute the essence of God" and "express the essence of God" just mean: "is identical with the essence of God"? Does one attribute alone constitute and express the essence of God or does the constitution and expression of God require all the attributes? We will need answers to these questions in order to solve the problem of how to interpret Spinoza's conception of the essence of God.

Problem three: the true conception of God

What is the true conception of God? That is, what is it to have a true idea of God? Is the true conception of God simply the conception of the attributes?[4] If this is the case, then we must ask whether the true conception of God is the conception of one attribute, the collection of attributes, or the totality of attributes.

In 2p47 Spinoza claims that the human intellect has an adequate idea of the essence of God:

> 2p47: The human Mind has an adequate knowledge of God's eternal and infinite essence.[5]

By 2d2 we know that when the essence of a thing is conceived the thing is necessarily conceived. So, given 2p47 we know that the human intellect has an adequate idea of God. In the scholium of 2p1 Spinoza says that we can conceive God through one attribute alone:

> 2p1s: So since we can conceive an infinite Being by attending to thought alone, Thought (by 1D4 and D6) is necessarily one of God's infinite attributes, as we maintained.

Hence, it seems that the human intellect can have an adequate idea of God through one attribute alone, regardless of whether God is identical with one attribute, the collection of attributes, or the totality of attributes.[6]

However, no attribute can be conceived through another, by 1p10:

> Each attribute of a substance must be conceived through itself.

This information raises problems for the view that God is somehow identical with the attributes. If God is identical with an attribute God can be conceived through that attribute, but this either leaves one other attribute (at the least) unaccounted for, or it suggests that there is more than one substance, which is an impossibility according to 1p14.[7] If, on the other hand, God is identical with the collection of attributes, then either God is inconceivable (since God is conceivable through any given attribute alone, yet no other attribute can be conceived through any given attribute) or the other attributes *are* conceivable through one attribute (i.e. the collection is conceivable via one attribute), yet this view directly contradicts 1p10. Finally, if God is identical with the totality of attributes, then either God is inconceivable (since God is conceivable through any given attribute alone, but the totality of attributes cannot be conceived through any given attribute) or the other attributes are conceivable through one attribute (i.e. the totality is conceivable via one attribute), which again contradicts 1p10. None of these scenarios is consistent with the text. A satisfactory solution to this problem must be found in order to explain what a true conception of God is (i.e. of what it consists) and how the human intellect has that idea.

Now that we understand the ramifications of three of the main problems to be discussed, let us turn to the consideration of views held by contemporary Spinoza scholars on the subject of God and the attributes. This will set a foundation for the resolution of the three problems.

Chapter 2

The "God Is the Thing that Has Attributes and Modes as Properties" Interpretation

Jonathan Bennett's interpretation

Jonathan Bennett understands Spinoza to claim that substances are "things" that have properties; and Spinoza's substance is the ultimate subject because God is the one and only logically and causally self-sufficient entity of which all other being is predicated.[1] There are two kinds of properties of God on Bennett's interpretation, viz. modes and attributes, the attributes being the "absolutely basic and irreducible properties" of God.[2] Attributes, according to Bennett, are "ways of being" for God. That is, God may be understood as being an extended thing or being a thinking thing, etc. Regarding the number of attributes, Bennett thinks it possible that they total only two.[3]

Although Bennett claims that, for Spinoza, the attributes are the basic *properties* of substance he also says that the only difference between substance and attribute is that they are different *presentations* of the content of only one thing, i.e. substance is the substantival presentation and attribute is the adjectival presentation of one entity.[4] What does this mean? Bennett answers:

> The difference between size-shape-location (or for short, *extension*) and the thing which has those properties (that is, *extended substance*) is not one of content but just of logical form. . . . We use the concept of substance to think of what has the attribute, and we use the concept of attribute to think of what the substance has; but it is the same conceptual content in each case.[5]

Presumably, it is not substance and attributes themselves that are presentations of one thing. Rather, Bennett seems to be claiming that the *concept* of substance and the *concept* of attribute are two different concepts that present (to the intellect) the content of one thing in two different ways; i.e. the concept "attribute" is the presentation of the unique entity as extension or thought, etc., and the concept "substance" is the presentation of the unique entity as "*that which has* . . . extension or thought or whatever".[6] Bennett says that the notion of "that which has attributes" adds nothing to the conceptual content of an attribute.

One might conclude that Bennett thinks that substance and attribute are the same thing. That is, if the content of the concept of substance and the content of the concept of attribute is the same, then the only difference appears to be in the manner of conception itself. When one thinks of substance one thinks of what has attributes, and when one thinks of attributes one thinks of what substance has. In either case, however, one is thinking of the exact same content, i.e. "substance" and "attribute" are terms that denote the same entity.

It seems that one could consider this view to be subjectivist in nature. That is, if the only difference between God and the attributes is conceptual then the attributes might be viewed as a product of the intellect, i.e. a method of thinking about God that renders God intelligible to the intellect. So, one might argue that on this view the attributes do not have objective existence and hence this is a form of subjectivism. On the other hand, one might consider this a bundle theory. To avoid being a bundle theorist one must claim that a thing is not identical with its properties. However, Bennett thinks that the conceptual content of the idea of an attribute is the same as the conceptual content of the idea of substance; the only difference is in the *way* the content is conceived. If this is true then it might be argued that one is thinking of the same *thing* in either case. Hence, God must be identical with one, both, or all of the attributes. One might therefore argue that the thing (God) is identical with its properties (the attributes) and so this is a bundle theory.

Bennett avoids both the conclusion that the attributes are subjective in nature and the conclusion that God and the attributes are identical. Bennett holds that although "substance" and "attribute" are different ways of referring to the same entity, God is not the attributes. For Bennett, the attributes really do exist (as ways of being for God) but God is neither a particular attribute nor the collection of the attributes.[7] The problem of the relation between God and the attributes is addressed by Bennett's theory of the essence of God. Bennett claims that "God" and "attribute" both apply to an entity that is of a nature that spans the attributes. The attributes are not the essence of God; rather, the essence of God is all or part of the trans-attribute differentiae that are expressed through the attributes.

The trans-attribute differentiae that are expressed through each attribute are modes. *These* modes, however, are not what we generally think of when we think of modes in Spinoza's ontology. We may speak of the mind of a particular individual as a thinking mode, i.e. a mode under the attribute of thought, and we may speak of the body of a particular individual as an extended mode, i.e. a mode under the attribute of extension. Under Bennett's interpretation these are not modes, strictly speaking.

Bennett says, "The attributes let the essence [of God] 'come through', so to speak."[8] Under this interpretation of the essence of God, a thinking mode is not a mode in the strict sense. Instead, a thinking mode is the *expression* of a particular mode, e.g. mode A, as a thinking thing. Mode A also is expressed (as an extended thing) under the attribute of extension. It follows that distinct mode B is expressed as a thinking thing through the attribute of thought, and mode B is expressed as an extended thing through the attribute of extension. The same is the case for every other mode; all modes are expressed through every attribute. Indeed, in 2p7s Spinoza claims that a mode comprehended under the attribute of extension and the idea of that mode comprehended under the attribute of thought are one and the same mode *expressed* in different ways.[9]

The modes, then, according to Bennett, are not things comprehended under the attributes themselves. Rather, the modes are entities that are in a sense *beyond yet expressed through* each attribute. Bennett claims that because of this aspect of Spinoza's metaphysics there necessarily is something that spans the attributes, something other than the expressions under the attributes. The modes, then, are entities that span the attributes; the modes are the trans-attribute differentiae. That is, every mode is expressed through every attribute; hence, according to Bennett, there must be entities (modes) that are different from their expressions under the attributes. These individual modes are not in the attributes; rather, they are the entities that span (and are expressed through) the attributes.

Bennett and the three problems

For Bennett, although "God" and "attribute" are terms that relate to the same entity, God and the attributes are not identical.[10] God and attribute are two different concepts that describe only one thing. The attributes are ways of being for God that render the essence of God (the trans-attribute differentiae, i.e. modes) intelligible to the intellect. That is Bennett's response to problem number one—that regarding the relation of God to the attributes. In answer to problem number two—that regarding the essence of God—Bennett claims that there are two senses of the term "essence of God" in Spinoza: the 2d2 sense of "necessary and sufficient condition for existence" and the sense in which the essence of God is "either the whole truth about God or some part of it which is logico-causally sufficient for the rest".[11] This "source of the whole truth" about God on Bennett's account is all or part of the system of trans-attribute differentiae. While the attributes are not the "source of the whole truth" about God on this account of Spinoza's God, the attributes nevertheless play a vital role by functioning as the route of accessibility to the intellect. The system of trans-attribute differentiae is expressed through the attributes, and it is this expression that the intellect comprehends. In response to problem number three—that concerning the true conception of God—Bennett claims that the human intellect perceives the essence of God through the attributes. Moreover, Bennett says that "what the intellect perceives of a substance as constituting its essence" in 1d4 is just the right expression.[12] That is, according to Bennett, the human intellect cannot conceive the essence of God directly since the human intellect cannot conceive the modes in abstraction from the attributes.[13] Instead, the human intellect perceives the essence of God by comprehending the trans-attribute differentiae *expressed* as thinking and as extended. That is, since the intellect cannot conceive the modes in abstraction from the attributes the intellect instead perceives the trans-attribute differentiae (i.e. the essence of God) via the attributes through which they are expressed.

In conclusion, for Bennett God is *the thing that has attributes and modes as properties*; the essence of God is *the trans-attribute differentiae* (or the modes in abstraction from the attributes); and the attributes are *the ways of being for God* that express the trans-attribute modes.

Discussion

Bennett presents an engaging interpretation of God and the attributes in Spinoza. Bennett claims that God is the substantival presentation and attribute is the adjectival presentation of *one* entity. Hence, one might conclude that God and attribute are the same thing. It is clear, however, that on Bennett's interpretation the attributes are neither identical with God nor subjective in nature. The attributes have objective existence as distinct ways of being for God.[14] Bennett explains that the intellect is not capable of conceiving the trans-attribute differentiae apart from their expressions through the attributes. Hence, for the intellect, the attributes *are* the presentation of God insofar as they are what the intellect perceives as constituting God's essence. Bennett claims that Spinoza's understanding of attribute as explicated in Letter 9 entails "an emptiness about the difference between substance and attribute".[15] Whether or not this is true, it should be clear that Bennett's interpretation of Spinoza's metaphysics does not result in any emptiness about the difference between the two. Indeed, although the terms "God" and "attribute" are different concepts that relate to one entity, the entity God and the attributes (as ways of being) *are* different. God is the unique entity of which everything else is predicated and the attributes are the ways of being for God, i.e. the ways the essence of God is expressed. So, on Bennett's view God is not the attributes; i.e. God is neither an attribute, nor the collection of attributes, nor the totality of attributes.

On Bennett's interpretation there are two senses of "the essence of God". First there is the 2d2 sense. A difficulty with Bennett's view is in understanding what God's essence is in the 2d2 sense. This is an important point, since most commentators on Spinoza generally consider 2d2 to be a pivotal point when discussing the essence of God. 2d2 states that when that which pertains to the essence of a thing is conceived the thing itself is conceived, and when the thing is conceived that which pertains to the essence of the thing is conceived. One might suggest that this sounds as though a thing and its essence are identical, and that Spinoza is simply taking the time to make that fact clear in 2d2. Bennett, however, says that it is because Spinoza omits discussion of "property" in his definition of essence that one might consider this reading of 2d2. Indeed, Bennett says that to read 2d2 as a claim that the essence of X is X renders the definition vacuous. If we agree with Bennett on this point and read 2d2 not as vacuous but as meaningful, then it seems that for Spinoza a thing must not be identical with its essence. However, given what Bennett says about the trans-attribute differentiae and the attributes, it is unclear what the essence of God is in the 2d2 sense. Bennett reads 2d2 as a claim by Spinoza that the essence of a thing is the qualitative "necessary and sufficient condition for existence", or that *property* which is unique to the thing.[16] Perhaps the 2d2 sense of the essence of God for Bennett is "having the attributes and modes as properties".

On Bennett's view, in addition to the 2d2 sense of God's essence there also is the "source of the whole truth" sense of the essence of God, according to which the essence of God is all or part of the system of trans-attribute differentiae. The trans-attribute differentiae are *expressed* through the attributes. According to Bennett, the human intellect is not capable of conceiving the trans-attribute differentiae as abstracted from the attributes, so the intellect perceives the essence of God (the trans-attribute differentiae) through the attributes. Therefore, the human intellect has an idea of the essence of God.

These two senses of "the essence of God" lead to a problem with Bennett's view regarding the human intellect and the adequate idea of the essence of God. On Bennett's interpretation God is the thing that has the attributes and modes as properties. Further, it seems that, for Bennett, the 2d2 sense of "the essence of God" would be "having the attributes and modes as properties", whereas the essence of God in the "source of the whole truth about God" sense is the trans-attribute differentiae. For Bennett, then, God and God's essence (in either sense) are not identical. That is, God (the thing that has attributes and modes as properties) is not identical with God's essence in the first sense (*having* the attributes and modes as properties), nor is God (the thing that has attributes and modes as properties) identical with the second sense of the essence of God (the trans-attribute differentiae).

If the meaning of 2d2 is as Bennett suggests, then a thing and its essence are not identical. If this is true, and the essence of God is not identical with God, then it might be argued that while the human intellect has an adequate idea of the essence of God, the human intellect does not have an adequate idea of God on Bennett's view. However, Bennett could claim that, though the essence of a thing is not identical with the thing, 2d2 shows that the idea of the essence of a thing necessarily results in the idea of the thing. Hence, there is an intimate and necessary connection between a thing and its essence such that the conception of the essence of God necessarily results in the conception of God. However, given that a thing is conceived through its essence, the human intellect must conceive God through God's essence. Yet, the human intellect cannot conceive God's essence (the trans-attribute differentiae),[17] and so it would seem that the human intellect does not have an adequate idea of God on Bennett's view. Since the human intellect is incapable of conceiving the modes in abstraction from the attributes, Bennett would have to argue that the human intellect conceives God through the 2d2 sense of the essence of God. However, conceiving the essence of God as "having the attributes and modes as properties" does not seem to result in the conception of an entity whose deeper essence is the trans-attribute differentiae. Indeed, on Bennett's interpretation the human intellect cannot conceive these modes. It seems, then, that conceiving the attributes—which are not the essence of God according to Bennett—is the closest the human intellect can get to the conception of the deepest essence of God—which is the modes in abstraction from the attributes; and, hence, conceiving the attributes is the closest the human intellect can get to an adequate conception of God.

This problem would seem to be enough to make us reconsider the view that the most basic properties of God are modes that span the attributes and that the essence of God is impossible to conceive even for the infinite intellect.[18] Michael Della Rocca argues convincingly against Bennett's view on the essence of God by pointing out that in 1p28d Spinoza says that modes "are nothing but affections of God's attributes".[19] For this reason Della Rocca claims that there can be no modes in abstraction from the attributes. Further, Della Rocca argues that this view cannot be right because Bennett claims that the infinite intellect is incapable of conceiving the modes in abstraction from the attributes. Della Rocca shows that this claim is inconsistent with the text since all of God's ideas are true and so "Bennett must be wrong in saying that for Spinoza, God is mistaken about God's own essence".[20]

Chapter 3

The "God Is the Collection of Attributes" Interpretation

Edwin Curley's interpretation

Edwin Curley takes seriously Spinoza's declarations that he means the same by God and attribute. Spinoza appears to make the claim that God and attribute are identical in the demonstration of 1p4.[1] Also, in Letter 9 Spinoza states:

> By substance I understand what is in itself and is conceived through itself, i.e., whose concept does not involve the concept of another thing. I understand the same by attribute, except that it is called attribute in relation to the intellect, which attributes such and such a definite nature to substance.

With these statements and others in mind, Curley claims that Spinoza identifies God with the attributes.[2] On this view the attribute of thought or extension alone is not, however, identical with God. For Curley the attributes are *actually infinite* in number,[3] and he claims that Spinoza "does identify substance with its attribute, or rather, with the totality of its attributes. . . . So substance is not . . . a distinct entity. It is the attributes themselves"[4]— "For substance simply *is* the sum of its attributes."[5]

Curley believes that the identification of God with the collection of the attributes may explain Spinoza's meaning in his reference to "God, or all of God's attributes" in 1p19 and 1p20c. Also, this identity may explain why Spinoza sometimes refers to modes as caused by or as the result of an attribute of God.[6] That is, if God *is* the collection of the attributes then Spinoza may rightfully refer to a mode either as caused by God or as caused by an attribute or attributes of God.

Curley's interpretation of God as the collection of the attributes seems to be a kind of bundle theory.[7] A bundle theory about substances is a view that any individual substance is simply a collection of all and only the qualities had by that particular thing.[8] Thus, a substance can be *identified* with the sum of its qualities.[9] Hence, a bundle theorist may claim that a substance and the sum of its qualities are one and the same; i.e. a substance and the sum of its qualities are absolutely identical entities. It seems, then, that there is no "thing" that has qualities. The "thing" is simply the qualities themselves, taken collectively.[10]

Curley and the three problems

With regard to the problem of the relation between God and the attributes, Curley holds the view that the relation between God and the attributes is one of identity. On Curley's view, God is not identical with any particular attribute; rather, God is identical with the sum of the distinct attributes.[11] With regard to the problem of the essence of God, Curley claims that the attributes are the essence of God. Indeed, Curley says that Spinoza uses the following expressions equivalently: God, God's nature, God's power, the laws of God's nature, and God's attributes.[12] Curley, however, thinks that God has two kinds of essences. First, for Curley, *each particular attribute* constitutes *an* essence of God: "Since these attributes are supposed to be really distinct from each other . . . perhaps we should say that each constitutes *an* essence of the one substance."[13] Curley states the point clearly in the following passage:

> We know, therefore, that there can be no absurdity in supposing that a being has more than one attribute, i.e., more than one essence. And if God is truly infinite, truly without any limitations whatever, we cannot suppose that he has only some finite number of attributes. So our conception of God as supremely perfect forces us to accept as legitimate the conception of a being possessing infinitely many attributes or essences.[14]

Hence, Curley says that God has more than one essence; indeed, on Curley's view God has infinitely many essences. Secondly, for Curley, *the collection of attributes* constitutes *the* essence of God: "God's essence, i.e. the totality of his attributes, is eternal (P19) and immutable (P20C2)".[15] Finally, with regard to the problem of the true conception of God, Curley thinks that the human intellect has an adequate idea of the essence of God via any particular attribute. That is, since each attribute is *an* essence of God and the collection of attributes is *the* essence of God, it is through the attributes that the human intellect has an idea of the essence of God.

In conclusion, for Curley God is *the collection of attributes*, the essence of God is *the collection of attributes*, and the attributes are *essences of God* (i.e. each particular attribute is an essence of God).

Discussion

Curley presents an interesting interpretation of God and the attributes in Spinoza. Curley claims that both God and the essence of God are the collection of attributes. Curley's notion of the essence of God is expanded by his claim that while the sum of distinct attributes is *the* essence of God, particular attributes are essences of God; that is, each attribute is *an* essence of God. By 2d2 we know that when the essence of a thing is conceived the thing is conceived; so if the essence of the collection of attributes is conceived then the collection of the attributes is conceived. So, on Curley's view, the human intellect has access to God and God's essence via either the attribute of thought or the attribute of extension.

The interpretation of both God and the essence of God as the sum of distinct attributes raises a question regarding 1d4, Spinoza's definition of attribute:

> By attribute I understand what the intellect perceives of a substance, as constituting its essence.

If God is the collection of the attributes, then does each attribute constitute the essence of the collection of the attributes, or does it take the entire collection of the attributes to constitute their collective essence?[16]

In the first case each attribute constitutes the essence of the collection of distinct attributes. So the intellect can conceive the essence of the collection of the attributes via one attribute.[17] However, if the collection of the attributes can be conceived through any particular attribute, then that attribute must be the other attributes, since (by 1p10) no attribute can be conceived through another.[18] So there cannot be many attributes but only one. This, however, cannot be right since we know that there are at least two attributes, viz. thought and extension. It seems, then, that since no other attribute can be conceived via a particular attribute, no attribute can constitute the essence of the collection of distinct attributes. So a particular attribute alone cannot be conceived by the intellect as that which constitutes the essence of the collection of the attributes.[19]

In the second case it takes the collection of the attributes to constitute the essence of the collection of distinct attributes. So the intellect must conceive the essence of the collection of the attributes via the collection of the attributes. But if there are more than two attributes then a problem arises. The human intellect, according to Spinoza, is incapable of conceiving more than two attributes, viz. thought and extension. Hence, if there are more than two attributes, then the human intellect must be incapable of conceiving the essence of God, i.e. the collection of distinct attributes.

It might, therefore, be argued that Spinoza must have been referring in 1d4 to the infinite intellect, rather than the finite intellect, since the infinite intellect is capable of conceiving the collection of the attributes regardless of how many there are.[20] However, whether the intellect in 1d4 is finite or infinite or both makes no difference in this case since Spinoza claims (in 2p47) that the human mind *does* have an adequate idea of the eternal and infinite essence of God via the attributes. That is, according to 2p45:

> Every idea of any body or particular thing existing in actuality necessarily involves the eternal and infinite essence of God.[21]

According to the demonstration of 2p45, because every idea has God as its cause, every idea necessarily involves the essence of God (since, by 1a4, the idea of an effect involves the idea of its cause and, by 1p15, everything is caused by God).[22] Further, in 2p46 Spinoza says:

> The knowledge of God's eternal and infinite essence which each idea involves is adequate and perfect.

The demonstration of 2p46 refers to 2p38:

> Those things which are common to all, and which are equally in the part and in the whole, can only be conceived adequately.

Spinoza states in 2p46d that what gives knowledge of the essence of God is equally in the part and in the whole.[23] So, every idea involves the adequate and perfect knowledge of the essence of God. Indeed, 2p47 states:

> The human Mind has an adequate knowledge of God's eternal and infinite essence.

The human mind has ideas. God's causation is common to all things, hence every idea involves the essence of God. Whatever is common to all things is adequately conceived, so the knowledge of God's essence is necessarily adequate and perfect. Therefore, every human mind has an adequate idea of the essence of God. So, if God is identical with the collection of the attributes, then the human intellect must have an adequate idea of the essence of the collection of the attributes.

If there are only two attributes, i.e. thought and extension, then it is clear that the human intellect can conceive the essence of the collection of the attributes. On Curley's interpretation God is identical with the essence of God. Therefore, if there are only two attributes, then the human intellect has an adequate idea of both God and the essence of God. However, if the quantity of attributes is infinite, as Curley claims, then it seems that the human intellect cannot have an adequate idea of either God or the essence of God (since the human intellect perceives only two attributes). So, if the attributes are infinite in number then the human intellect cannot have an adequate idea of the collection of distinct attributes. Also, I have shown above that the collection of attributes cannot be conceived via any particular attribute. This seems to be a problem for this view.

It must be noted, however, that (by 2p1s) the conception of more than one attribute is not necessary for the human intellect to have an adequate idea of God. Indeed, in 2p1s Spinoza tells us that we can conceive God through one attribute:

> So since we can conceive an infinite Being by attending to thought alone, Thought (by 1d4 and 1d6) is necessarily one of God's infinite attributes.

Spinoza has already proved in 1p14 and its demonstration that there exists only one substance and that substance is God:

> 1p14: Except God, no substance can be or be conceived.

Hence, the infinite being that is conceived through thought alone must be the unique infinite being, i.e. God. Moreover, Spinoza shows in 2p1 that thought is an attribute of God, i.e. the unique infinite being. So, the human intellect can have an adequate idea of God through the attribute of thought alone. Since the attributes are parallel in nature, it follows that the human intellect can have an adequate idea of God through the attribute of extension alone. That is, by 2p7, everything that is expressed under any particular attribute is also expressed under every other attribute.[24] Hence, if the human intellect can have an adequate idea of God via the attribute of thought, then the human intellect can have an adequate idea of God via any other attribute. So (by 2p1s, 2p7, and 2p47), the human intellect has an adequate idea of the essence of God through either the attribute of thought or the attribute of extension.

On Curley's view, God is the collection of the attributes, and the essence of God is the collection of the attributes. It seems, then, that Curley would support the position that the essence of a thing and the thing itself are identical entities. That is, if God is the collection of the attributes and the collection of the attributes is the essence of God, then God is identical with God's essence. Hence, when one conceives the essence of God one conceives God, and when one conceives God one conceives God's essence. According to 2p1s, one can conceive an infinite being, i.e. God, through the attribute of thought alone (or through any particular attribute alone). Hence, one can conceive God through the attribute of thought alone (or through any particular attribute alone).[25] If this is true and if God and God's essence are identical, then it seems that on Curley's view any particular attribute is God. Curley claims that there are indeed an infinite number of attributes. I have argued, however, that the view that God is identical with the collection of the attributes is incompatible with Spinoza's claim that one can adequately conceive God through one attribute alone.

An essence vs the essence of God

The foregoing arguments have been raised on the understanding that God is one entity, and an entity of one essence. This, however, is not exactly the view that Curley espouses. Instead, Curley suggests that God is a complex entity that is composed of special elements, i.e. the attributes.[26] The elements are special because every attribute necessarily exists and each attribute is conceived only through itself. On this view no attribute constitutes *the* essence of God; rather, each attribute constitutes *an* essence of God. The result of this stance is that God has many essences.[27]

The view of God as an entity with many essences may serve as a way out of the problem of how to interpret 1d4. Curley claims that any particular attribute is *an* essence of God, and that the collection of particular attributes is *the* essence of God.[28] 1d4 says that by attribute we are to understand "what the intellect perceives of a substance, as constituting its essence". If "its essence" means *the* essence of a substance, then 1d4 may be interpreted as meaning that any particular attribute is perceived by the intellect as constituting *the* essence of God. In this case (since the essence of God is identical with God, on Curley's interpretation [29]) any particular attribute may be perceived as God. But this cannot be right since, on Curley's interpretation, God is not identical with any particular attribute. On the other hand, if "its essence" means *an* essence, then there is no problem with Curley's interpretation relative to 1d4. In this case, any particular attribute is perceived by the intellect as constituting *an* essence of God. On this interpretation no particular attribute is identical with God.

Although Curley's complex notion of the essence of God may avoid problems with the interpretation of 1d4, there are other issues regarding this view of God and the attributes. Curley wants to claim that God has more than one essence. In fact, on Curley's interpretation God has as many essences as there are attributes. The essence of a thing may be interpreted in at least two ways. It may be viewed as identical with the thing itself, or, alternatively, as *not* identical with the thing itself. If a thing and its essence *are* identical then it seems that, on Curley's interpretation, God must be many entities (since God has many essences). Certainly, if God is many entities then there exists more than one substance. However, given 1d6 and 1p14 it is impossible that more than one substance exists:

> 1d6: By God I understand a being absolutely infinite, i.e., a substance consisting of an infinity of attributes, of which each one expresses an eternal and infinite essence.

> 1p14: Except God, no substance can be or be conceived.

There does not seem to be any textual evidence in support of the view that God has many essences (and hence is many entities). Indeed, Spinoza says that even though the attributes of thought and extension are conceived to be really distinct, we cannot deduce from that fact that they constitute two entities.[30]

On the second alternative a thing and its essence are *not* identical. This might result in the possibility of a thing having more than one essence and still not being many entities. On Curley's view the *collection of attributes* is *the* essence of God while any *particular attribute*, on the other hand, is *an* essence of God. So the particular attributes are, it seems, essences of parts of the essence of God. That is, if God's essence is a *collection* of special *elements*, i.e. the attributes, and an attribute is *an* essence of God rather than *the* essence of God, then the attributes must be partial essences of the whole essence. In other words, an attribute is *an* essence of *the* essence of God.

So, if God is an entity whose essence is the collection of the attributes and the particular attributes are essences of God, then either God is many entities (if any particular essence is identical with a particular thing),[31] or God has many partial essences (if any particular essence is not identical with a particular thing). It seems that the interpretation of God's essence as identical with the collection of attributes results in problems regarding the adequate conception of the essence of God by the human intellect. Whatever God is, the human intellect must adequately conceive the essence of that entity in order to have an adequate idea of God.[32] If God is many entities, then the human intellect must conceive the many essences in order to have an adequate idea of God. If, on the other hand, God is one entity that has many partial essences then the human intellect may have an adequate idea of the essence of God through any particular attribute.[33] On this understanding of the adequate conception of God, the human intellect has an adequate idea of *an* essence of God. However, God appears to be an entity whose essence is made up of parts, i.e. the attributes are parts of the collection of the attributes.

In either case, the human intellect can conceive only two attributes, thought and extension. Hence, it might be claimed that either the human intellect does not have an adequate idea of God (if the quantity of attributes is infinite) or there are only two attributes and so the human intellect does have an adequate idea of God. However, recall that the human intellect can conceive God through one attribute alone. Therefore, either God and the collection of the attributes (whether there are two or more) are not identical entities or one attribute is *the* essence of God rather than *an* essence of God. But, if any particular attribute is *the* essence of

God then any particular attribute and God are identical entities. And if *every* particular attribute is *the* essence of God then God and every attribute are identical entities. Hence, there can exist only one attribute that is the essence of God. But we know that there are at least two attributes, so it seems that neither a particular attribute nor the collection of attributes can be the essence of God, if God is identical with God's essence.

A further problem lies in Curley's understanding of God as the collection of attributes. If God is the collection of distinct attributes, then it seems that God is composed of parts. Yet, we know by 1p12 and 1p13 that God is neither a divisible entity nor composed of parts:

> 1p12: No attribute of a substance can be truly conceived from which it follows that the substance can be divided.

> 1p13: A substance which is absolutely infinite is indivisible.

Bennett agrees that Curley's view makes God into an entity consisting of parts: he says, "But the only sense we can attach to this involves treating the substance as an aggregate, a collection with members or a complex with parts."[34]

Alan Donagan's interpretation

For Alan Donagan, though the number of attributes may be many or few, one thing is certain: an attribute is that by which the essence of God is truly known.[35] In 1d4 Spinoza explains that the attributes are that by which the intellect perceives the essence of God. Further, by 1a6 and the demonstration of 2p32 the attributes must be the *true* presentation of the essence of God:

> 1a6: A true idea must agree with its object.

> 2p32d: For all ideas which are in God agree entirely with their objects (by P7C), and so (by IA6) they are all true, q.e.d.

Hence the idea of an attribute is a true idea of the presentation of the essence of God.

Donagan claims that an attribute that constitutes the essence of a substance may be identical with that substance.[36] However, this is true only in case the substance, e.g. substance A, is a substance of only one attribute. In this case the attribute of A determines both the being of the substance and its *kind*. Hence, the attribute that constitutes the essence of A is identical with the essence of A (and the essence of A is identical with A).[37] The attribute of substance A is, therefore, identical with substance A. This is not the case, however, regarding a substance of more than one attribute. That is, according to Donagan, if substance B has more than one attribute, then no attribute of B can be identical with the essence of B. Hence, no one attribute of B can be identical with B. This is the case, Donagan says, because a single attribute of B determines its being but only one of its *kinds*. Hence, no one attribute of substance B can be identical with the essence of substance B, "because, although it determines its being, it determines only one of its kinds, and not those determined by its other attributes".[38]

Donagan and the three problems

It seems that Donagan's response to the problem of the relation of God to the attributes would be to claim that no particular attribute is identical with God, since God is an entity of more than one attribute. However, Donagan says that the attribute of a substance of only one attribute is identical with the essence of that substance and hence with that substance. One might conclude from this that Donagan would claim that the collection of attributes of a substance of more than one attribute is identical with the essence of that substance, and hence with that substance, i.e. the collection of attributes determines both the being of the substance and all of its kinds. Hence, one might conclude that, for Donagan, God is identical with the collection of attributes. In answer to problem two—that of the essence of God—it seems that the collection of the attributes of God must be the essence of God on Donagan's view.[39] Interestingly, though, Donagan claims that any *particular* attribute fulfills the stipulations of 2d2.[40] That is, when any particular attribute is given, God is given, and when any particular attribute is taken away, God is taken away. The attributes, then, *pertain to* the essence of God, though no particular attribute is *identical* with God. Clearly, Donagan does not take 2d2 to be the definition of the essence of a thing. Instead, Donagan says that 2d2 defines "the expression 'belonging to' as it applies to essence".[41] Regarding the problem of the true conception of God, Donagan thinks that the human intellect perceives the essence of God through any particular attribute. However, Donagan does say that each attribute expresses the essence of God only in its own kind, i.e. there are as many kinds of expressions of the essence of God as there are attributes.

Discussion

There are concerns about Donagan's stance on each of the three problems. First, there is a concern about the divisibility of a substance. For Donagan each attribute constitutes and expresses the essence of God, though only in its own kind. It seems that if Donagan were to claim that God is identical with the attributes, then God must be identical with the collection of *all* of the attributes, i.e. it could not be the case that God is identical with the collection of only some of the attributes. Hence, Donagan would hold the "God is the collection of attributes" view. This interpretation seems to construe God as an entity that is made up of distinct *parts*, i.e. the distinct attributes. This is a problem since God is an indivisible being, and hence cannot be made up of parts.[42] One might try to avoid this problem by claiming that the attributes are merely *conceptually* distinct from one another, although they are not ontologically distinct. Hence, one could claim that God is not made up of really distinct parts. However, if the human intellect conceives the attributes truly, then the attributes are really distinct from one another.[43]

There also is a problem regarding the essence of God on Donagan's interpretation. Donagan claims that an attribute is that by which the essence of God is truly known, yet it seems that each attribute allows knowledge of the essence of God only in that kind. Therefore, according to Donagan, a particular attribute is not identical with God. Donagan makes it clear, however, that this does not mean that God has more than one essence. Indeed, Donagan claims that the essence of God is the essence of an individual and hence the essence of God is an individual, i.e. the essence of an individual is not a multiplicity, it is one.[44] In addition, the attributes are not properties; rather, they too are individuals. So, for Donagan, the attributes are individual presentations of one essence, i.e. the essence of God. That is, "since God has only one essence, the eternal and infinite essences which (by E.,I, Def.6) God's diverse attributes express must all be identical with that essence and therefore with one another".[45] However, if the essences of the diverse attributes are the same, then the attributes are the same.

Donagan does not plainly state whether one attribute alone is adequate for the true conception of the essence of God. In 2d2 Spinoza states that that which pertains to the essence of a thing is that which, when it is given, the thing is necessarily posited, and when it is taken away the thing is necessarily taken away. Donagan does claim that the attributes *pertain* to the essence of God.[46] That is, Donagan says the attribute of extension expresses an eternal and infinite essence. The same is the case for every other attribute. Hence, if extension is given, then an absolutely infinite being is given and if extension is taken away, then an absolutely infinite being is necessarily taken away; the same follows for any other attribute. According to Donagan, then, each attribute pertains to the essence of God, and the essence expressed by each attribute is identical with the essence of God. It would appear, therefore, that although one attribute expresses the essence of God only in that kind, Donagan must conclude that one attribute is adequate for the true conception of the essence of God (since, on Donagan's view, for Spinoza the essence expressed by each particular attribute is identical with the essence of God).

One might suggest that, on Donagan's interpretation, one attribute is not only adequate for the true conception of the essence of God, but one attribute is *identical* with the essence of

God, and hence one attribute is identical with God. This conclusion can be drawn by considering the particular claims in Donagan's interpretation of God and the attributes. Donagan says:

> What constitutes an essence may be identical with that essence, and so with its substance, but it need not be. The attribute constituting the essence of a substance of one attribute is identical with it; for it determines not only the being of that substance, but also its kind. No attribute of a substance of more than one attribute, however, can be identical with its essence, because, although it determines its being, it determines only one of its kinds, and not those determined by its other attributes.[47]

Previously, the conclusion was drawn that on Donagan's view the collection of the attributes is identical with the essence of God, and hence the collection of attributes is identical with God. That is, according to the above quotation, the attribute of a substance of only one attribute is identical with the essence of that substance, and hence with that substance. In this case, the substance is identical with its essence. One can draw the further conclusion that the entire collection of attributes of a substance of more than one attribute must be identical with the essence of that substance, since they collectively determine the being of that substance *and* all of its kinds. Since, on Donagan's interpretation, the essence of a substance of one attribute is identical with that substance, it seems that the essence of a substance of more than one attribute is identical with that substance. Since the attribute of a substance of one attribute is identical with the essence of that substance (and so with that substance), it seems to follow that the entire collection of attributes of a substance of more than one attribute is identical with the essence of that substance (and so with that substance). So it seems that, on Donagan's interpretation, God is identical with the collection of attributes.

In the above quotation Donagan says that for Spinoza no attribute of a substance of more than one attribute can be identical with its essence. In his earlier work, however, Donagan says that for Spinoza the essence expressed by any particular attribute is identical with the essence of God.[48] If it is true that on Donagan's interpretation God is identical with God's essence, then we must ask whether it is each particular attribute that is identical with God's essence or it is the collection of attributes that is identical with God's essence.

It seems legitimate to draw the conclusion (from the above quotation) that God is identical with God's essence, and that the essence of God is identical with the collection of attributes. The concern, of course, is Donagan's claim that the essence expressed by each particular attribute is identical with the essence of God. If each particular attribute is identical with the essence of God then the conclusion can be drawn that one attribute is identical with God. That is, on Donagan's interpretation, in the case of a substance of one attribute, the attribute of that substance is identical with the essence of that substance; hence the attribute is identical with the substance.[49] One can conclude, therefore, that if the essence expressed by one attribute of God is identical with the essence of God, then that one attribute is identical with God (since God is identical with God's essence). Indeed, the further conclusion can be drawn that one attribute is identical with the collection of attributes (since God is identical with God's essence, which is identical with the collection of attributes).

Donagan clarifies Spinoza's use of the terms "constitute" and "express".[50] Donagan says that Spinoza means the same thing when he uses the terms "constitute" and "express", except that by "express" Spinoza means "in a kind". If this is true, then, in 1d4, Spinoza means that by attribute he understands what constitutes the essence of God *completely*, i.e. any particular attribute constitutes the essence of God. There is therefore a conflict between Donagan's understanding of what an attribute constitutes and expresses and the interpretation of God as the collection of attributes. If any particular attribute satisfies the stipulation of 1d4, then (on Donagan's interpretation) any particular attribute must be identical with God.

For Donagan the collection of the attributes is both God and the essence of God. Hence, if one can conceive the essence of the collection of the attributes through one attribute, then one can conceive God via one attribute. But if God, i.e. the collection of the attributes, can be conceived through one attribute, then that one attribute must be the other attributes, since no attribute can be conceived through another. So there cannot be many attributes but only one. But this cannot be right, since we know that there are at least two attributes, viz. thought and extension. It seems, then, that the collection of attributes cannot be conceived through any particular attribute. So one attribute cannot be conceived by the intellect as that which constitutes the essence of the collection of the attributes.

Chapter 4

The "God Is the Totality of Attributes" Interpretation

H. F. Hallett's interpretation

H. F. Hallett understands Spinoza's God as the archetypal active entity. This action is not to be understood merely as those sequences of events that human minds perceive as occurring over time. Rather, Hallett understands the action of God as involving both *potency* and its *actuality*.[1] God is "a primordial infinite power" that necessarily has infinite and eternal effects; the action of this entity is determined by its own nature, which is absolutely indeterminate potency-in-act.[2] Indeed, God is the maximally active entity whose action is determined and whose effects are knowable; the effects of the maximally active entity are known by finite, durational human minds as infinitely variant types and degrees of being. God necessarily creates everything possible, for the action of God is "identical with perfect or absolute freedom".[3]

For Hallett, God is the maximally active entity whose existence involves no passivity. What does it mean for an entity to act? Spinoza claims in 3d2 that an entity may be understood as acting when it is the adequate cause of something that happens, i.e. when something follows *solely* from the nature of that entity.[4] Hallett clarifies agency as that which "involves both a power of *acting* and the expression of that power in something enacted".[5] Hence, God is the maximal agent, since by 1p16 absolutely everything follows from God's nature:

1p16: From the necessity of the divine nature there must follow infinitely many things in infinitely many modes, (i.e., everything which can fall under an infinite intellect.)

God, the original and ultimate agent, is an infinitely and eternally active entity whose action *necessarily* results in an infinite quantity of things that are caused by that action. That is, God necessarily involves not only the infinite and eternal *power* to act, but also infinite and eternal *action* itself. For, according to Hallett, "potency not 'in-act' is no potency".[6] Hence, God is *actual* power and not mere potentiality. That is, this causative being does not possess the mere potential to create; rather, this entity is necessarily eternally in the act of creating. God is an incessantly active creating agent; to wit, this agent is infinitely and eternally producing effects of every possible kind and to every possible degree, from the infinite immediate modes to the most privative examples of finitude.

Of the attributes Hallett says: "The attributes of Substance, then, are the essence of Substance as apprehended, and truly, by intellect: they do not *inhere* in it, but *constitute* its essence".[7] Hallett does not understand the attributes as properties or qualities possessed by God. The attributes do not inhere in God, nor are the attributes relative strictly to the human intellect, i.e. it is not the case that God lacks an infinite quantity of attributes; indeed, Hallett claims it is *not* paradoxical to say both that God consists of an infinity of attributes and that God is absolutely indeterminate.[8] Rather, Hallett's claim is that God and the attributes are *essentially* the same thing. When it comes to God and the attributes there is only one differentiating factor, according to Hallett, and that is intellect.[9] That is, in God the attributes are indiscerptible (i.e. the attributes are not separable from one another in God); it is only through the intellect that the attributes are discerptible.[10]

Hallett and the three problems

In response to the first problem—that regarding the relation between God and the attributes—Hallett claims that God is a *primordial infinite power*. God, however, is not ontologically distinct from the attributes. That is, the only differentiating factor between God and attribute is the intellect; *in God* the attributes are not distinct. Indeed, Hallett claims that "*substantial* Thought is identical with *substantial* Extension, *substantial* X, etc."[11] In response to problem number two—that regarding the essence of God—Hallett says that the attributes are the essence of God as apprehended truly by the intellect. Moreover, it is not the aggregate of attributes, but each attribute alone, which constitutes the essence of God.[12] Regarding problem number three—that concerning the true conception of God—Hallett claims both that there is no distinction of attributes in God, and that the intellect conceives the distinct attributes as the essence of God. The distinction of attributes, however, is relative only to the intellect and experience. Indeed, "it is the limitation of human nature as a mode of Thought and Extension alone that renders them discernible, though undivided and infinite in potency".[13] Not only does the intellect discern distinct attributes where no distinction in God exists, but the intellect also discerns an infinite number of attributes. Hallett, however, claims that God is by nature indeterminate, and involves no divisibility. Hence, there is no infinity of attributes in God.[14]

Discussion

There is a problem with Hallett's understanding of the relation between God, God's essence and the attributes. Hallett says that God is infinite and eternal indeterminate potency-in-act.[15] Further, Hallett claims that the essence of God is potency-in-act.[16] Finally, according to Hallett, the attributes are the essence of God as apprehended truly by the intellect.[17] So, God is potency-in-act, which is identical with the essence of God, and the attributes are the essence of God. Hence, God is identical with the attributes. On Hallett's view, however, the attributes are indiscerptible in God.[18] So, God is identical with the totality of indistinct (rather than the collection of distinct) attributes,[19] although each particular attribute constitutes the essence of God. How can God be identical with the indistinct attributes when the attributes are, by nature, distinct from one another?[20] That is, if the attributes are not conceived through one another (by 1p10), then they are not caused by one another (by 1a4), so they have nothing in common with one another (by 1p3); hence, the attributes are both conceptually and causally distinct from one another. Further, if the intellect apprehends the attributes truly, then (by 1a6) the attributes must be distinct from one another. If the attributes are distinct from one another, then they cannot be indistinct in God (for if they are, then the idea of the attributes is not a true idea).

In addition, Hallett's claim regarding the indiscerptibility of the attributes in God raises issues regarding the true conception of God by the human intellect. How is the idea of a particular distinct attribute the adequate idea of the essence of God, which is the indiscerptible attributes? That is, if the attributes are not ontologically distinct from one another, as Hallett claims, then how can the conception of an attribute as distinct from the other attributes be the adequate conception of the essence of God (which, according to Hallett, is the totality of indistinct attributes)? In other words, it seems as if a false conception, i.e. the conception of a distinct attribute, is supposed to deliver to the human intellect a true conception of the essence of God as the totality of indistinct attributes.

On Hallett's view, the separability of the attributes is relative only to the intellect, whereas in God no such distinction exists. This view seems untenable given Spinoza's claim in 1p10 and its demonstration that the attributes are conceived as really distinct from one another.[21] Hallett wants to claim that although the intellect conceives the attributes independently of one another, this is just a characteristic of the intellect and not of God. Hallett claims that in God the attributes are indistinguishable from one another *and* the intellect has a true conception of the attributes as distinct from one another. However, nowhere does Spinoza claim that God is an entity in which the distinct attributes are undiscoverable. Further, by 2p32, whatever the intellect conceives of God it conceives truly.[22] So, it seems impossible that the intellect's true conception of the attributes involves their distinction from one another while in God the attributes are indistinct from one another.

A further problem for this view is that given Hallett's claim that the only differentiating factor between God and the attributes is the intellect, it appears that Hallett's view may be understood as a subjectivist view—a view that the distinct attributes exist only in the intellect. Some, however, may claim that Hallett must be understood as holding an objectivist point of view since he does claim that the attributes exist, although they are indiscerptible in God.

The status of the attributes

This discussion of Hallett's stance on the attributes raises one of the main controversies regarding Spinoza's doctrine of the attributes of God: are the attributes subjective or objective in nature? The attributes are understood by some to be entirely subjective in nature. According to these commentators, the attributes do not actually exist in reality. Rather, the existence of the attributes is strictly relative to the intellect, as a function of and an aid to the intellect in its attempt to comprehend the essence of God. Others understand the attributes as objective in nature. These commentators claim that the attributes both exist in reality and constitute and express the essence of God.

Subjectivists claim that their position is supported by 1d4:

> By attribute I understand what the intellect perceives of a substance, as constituting its essence.

One who holds the subjectivist view may claim that in this definition (the definition of what an attribute *is*) Spinoza makes it clear that the existence of the attributes is relative only to the intellect. Some advance the argument further by claiming that "tanquam" in the Latin original of this definition is properly translated "as if", resulting in the attributes being perceived "as if" they constitute the essence of a substance, although they really don't. Subjectivists might also claim that support for their view is found in part of the demonstration of 1p4:

> Therefore, there is nothing outside the intellect through which a number of things can be distinguished from one another except substances, or what is the same (by D4), their attributes, and their affections, q.e.d.

Those who hold the subjectivist interpretation of the attributes may claim that what Spinoza thinks of the attributes is clear: there are only two categories of existing things, viz., substance(s) and modes. That the attributes are mentioned in this demonstration is of minor concern for the subjectivist since they are referred to according to their definition, 1d4. Hence, they may be understood, once again, as a way for the human intellect to perceive the essence of a substance.

Those who hold the objectivist point of view regarding the attributes often cite 1a6 as support for their stance. That is, by 2p47, the human intellect does have an adequate idea of the essence of God. Further, by 2p46, the idea of the essence of God is adequate and perfect; and, by 2p34, an adequate idea is a true idea.[23] Spinoza requires, in 1a6, that a true idea necessarily agree with its object. Therefore, the idea of the attributes, which is the idea of that which expresses the essence of God, is the idea of something that actually exists. For the attributes must exist independently of the intellect in order for the idea of the attributes to be a true idea, i.e. in order for the idea of the attributes to agree with its object. Hence, the attributes exist outside the intellect.

One of the main problems the objectivists face is the explanation of Spinoza's claims that there is nothing other than substance(s) and modes. It seems that, if there is nothing other than these two kinds of things, then one might be forced to claim that either the attributes are substances or modes, or the attributes do not actually exist. I will attempt to give a solution to this problem when I present my suggestion for the interpretation of the attributes of God. Discussion of these problems will automatically bring up questions regarding the "expression" and "constitution" of the essence of God. These issues will be examined in detail at that time.

Steven Parchment's interpretation

Steven Parchment is a contemporary commentator who holds a view similar to Hallett's. In a 1996 article, Parchment discusses the role of the attributes in Spinoza's metaphysics and their relation to the essence of God.[24] Parchment agrees in part with both the subjectivist and the objectivist positions on the attributes. Subjectivists hold that there are no attributes outside the intellect while objectivists claim that the attributes have their own reality apart from the intellect. Subjectivists often claim that Spinoza's reference to the intellect in 1d4 only serves to support their view that the attributes are created by the mind. Objectivists, on the other hand, maintain that the perceptions of the intellect relative to God are always true. Hence, objectivists claim that the particular attributes do exist outside the intellect and that an attribute constitutes the essence of God. Although Parchment sides with the objectivists insofar as they insist that the attributes *do* exist outside the intellect,[25] he agrees with the subjectivists who claim that "tanquam" in 1d4 should be translated "as if". Although the attributes exist, on this Parchmentian reading, no particular attribute constitutes the essence of God.[26] So, an attribute is only perceived by the intellect *as if* it constitutes the essence of God.

Parchment wants to avoid the common conclusion drawn by objectivists that God and the collection of distinct attributes are identical entities.[27] Indeed, Parchment understands Curley to hold the view that God is identical with the collection of particular attributes. A collection of particular attributes evokes the idea of a divisible entity, a different conception than that of an indivisible substance. Parchment claims that God, rather than being a collection of attributes, is a *unity* of all possible attributes, and that this unity of all the attributes is prior to the particular attributes. Indeed, "God is the ultimate indeterminate 'whole' which 'contains' specific attributes".[28] Further, "that totality cannot be the set of particular attributes discretely conceived, even if the set is infinite".[29] In fact, according to Parchment the true conception of any particular attributes *entails* the understanding that it is contained in an indivisible unity of attributes. Indeed, Parchment claims that his view "preserves the priority and indivisibility of God".[30] Parchment presents a view of God and the attributes in which God is the *totality* of attributes.[31]

In addition to his claim that God is not identical with a collection of distinct (or particular) attributes, Parchment also claims that the essence of God cannot be the collection of distinct attributes.[32] Rather, the essence of God is a unity such that the "attributes cannot be conceived as logically independent elements in the divine essence" because "the nature of God is said to consist in perfection and indeterminate being outside of any kind":[33] "God's essence can be constituted by infinite attributes and still be prior to any finite or infinite collection of individual attributes".[34] Whereas the essence of God can be constituted by the totality of indiscrete attributes, according to Parchment no particular attribute pertains to the essence of God:[35] "A particular attribute cannot pertain to or constitute the essence of God".[36] Further, Parchment claims that the attributes are not self-caused; rather, each attribute is a "logically posterior effect" of God.[37]

Descartes' theory of distinction

In order to understand Parchment's interpretation fully, it is necessary to understand his discussion of the Cartesian theory of distinction,[38] and its purported relevance to the question of the relation between God and the attributes in Spinoza. Parchment discusses Descartes' theory of distinction in some detail. He uses Descartes' theory to show that, for Spinoza, distinctions involve both the conception and the ontology of whatever is in question, e.g. the distinction between X and Y.[39] Hence, for Spinoza, when X and Y are really distinct (*distinctio realis*) X and Y are absolutely independent of one another. That is, neither the conception nor the existence of one involves the conception or existence of the other. When X and Y are modally distinct (*distinctio modalis*) there is a one-way dependence between X and Y. In other words, both the conception and existence of one depends on the conception and existence of the other, but not vice versa. Finally, when X and Y are merely conceptually distinct (*distinctio rationis*) X and Y are mutually dependent, i.e. when one is conceived the other is necessarily conceived. Indeed, Parchment says that "whatever things are mutually conceptually dependent must exist together, inseparably, in one and the same thing".[40] Hence, in the case of a *distinctio rationis*, "there is really only one existent thing".[41]

As a result of his discussion of the Cartesian theory of distinction, Parchment concludes that particular attributes are really distinct from one another, and hence that particular attributes are neither conceptually nor ontologically dependent on one another.[42] Although really distinct from one another, according to Parchment, the particular attributes are both conceptually and ontologically dependent on God.[43] God, on the other hand, is neither conceptually nor ontologically dependent on any of the particular attributes. Hence, Parchment concludes that God and the particular attributes are modally distinct. This entails that there exists only one conceptually and ontologically independent entity, i.e. God.

Parchment and the three problems

There are difficulties with Parchment's interpretation regarding each of the three problems. It is difficult to know where Parchment stands regarding the relations between God, the divine essence, and the totality of attributes (since he seems to claim both that these three are identical *and* that they are each conceptually distinct from one another). In addition, it is difficult to know what Parchment would consider to be an adequate idea of God; i.e. does the true conception of God result from the idea of a particular attribute, or does it result from the idea of the totality of attributes? I will attempt to uncover Parchment's stance on the three problems in order to see if Parchment's interpretation will shed light on Spinoza for us.

Parchment's answers to the three problems seem to hinge on a fundamental ambiguity about distinctions of reason and their relation to identity in his interpretation of God and the attributes. As a result of this ambiguity, there are two interpretive options concerning Parchment's stance. One possibility is that Parchment regards any X and Y that are distinguished only by reason as identical. In this case, although X and Y are conceptually distinct, they are identical.[44] The alternative possibility is that Parchment regards identity and distinctions of reason as mutually exclusive alternatives for any given X and Y. In this case, any X and Y that are identical are not distinguished from one another in any way; indeed, there is no conceptual distinction between X and Y. I will consider what Parchment's three answers to the three questions would be on both alternatives.

I will consider first the case in which things can be conceptually distinct and yet strictly identical. Does Parchment hold this view? Consider some of Parchment's statements. First, "The totality of attributes pertains to the divine essence (IP19D) and constitutes it (IP20D) and hence (by IID2) differs from it by a *distinctio rationis*".[45] Here Parchment claims that there is a conceptual distinction between *God's essence* and the *totality of attributes*. It could conceivably be doubted whether Parchment also says that there is a conceptual distinction between *God's essence* and *God*, but the following passage is at least some evidence that he draws such a distinction: "Since the divine essence has no limits and thus possesses the highest degree of reality, it follows (as Spinoza asserts) that God has the greatest power and thus infinite effects (IP16D)".[46] In this quote Parchment seems to be saying that there is a distinction (perhaps a conceptual distinction) between God's essence and God. This seems to be a reasonable assumption, since Cartesian practice (which Parchment wants to follow) requires us to say that a thing and its essence are conceptually distinct.

In addition to the distinction of reason between God's essence and the totality of attributes, and God's essence and God, Parchment says there is a conceptual distinction between *God* and the *totality of attributes*: "Although God as the *ens realissimum* is merely conceptually distinct from the totality of his attributes".[47] Hence, it seems that Parchment does think that God, God's essence, and the totality of the attributes are all conceptually distinct from one another. There is, however, another important quote that may indicate that Parchment indeed thinks that some X and Y can be both strictly identical and conceptually distinct: "God must be the logically prior unity of all possible attributes".[48] Here Parchment seems to be saying that God is identical with the totality of attributes. However, according to Parchment the totality of attributes is conceptually distinct from both God and the essence of God. There are, therefore, two possibilities. Either Parchment does think that things can be both strictly identical *and* conceptually distinct, or else his identity-ascribing remark ("God must be the logically prior unity of all possible attributes") is just a slip of the pen.

If the first possibility is the case, then, for Parchment, God *is* identical with the totality of attributes (although God is conceptually distinct from the totality of attributes). Since, on this view, a distinction of reason entails identity, the conclusion can be drawn that God is identical with God's essence, and the essence of God is identical with the totality of attributes. Hence, God is identical with God's essence, which is identical with the totality of attributes, which is identical with God.

If instead Parchment's remark identifying God with the totality of attributes is unintentional then he may hold the second interpretive option, i.e. identity and a distinction of reason are mutually exclusive alternatives for any given X and Y. So any X and Y that are identical are not distinguished from one another in any way; indeed, there is no conceptual distinction between X and Y. We know that, for Parchment, there is a conceptual distinction between God's essence and the totality of attributes,[49] and between God and the totality of attributes.[50] Further, it seems that Parchment claims there is a conceptual distinction between God's essence and God.[51] So God, God's essence, and the totality of attributes are all conceptually distinct from one another. Hence, none of these are identical with one another (since on this interpretive option any distinction between any X and Y rules out the possibility of identity between them).

The three problems and interpretive option one

I will now consider what Parchment's answers to the three problems would be on each of the interpretive options. Let's consider the first interpretive option—the case in which any X and Y that are distinguished only by reason are identical. On this interpretation,

God, God's essence, and the totality of attributes are strictly identical (although they are conceptually distinct). On this option it seems that Parchment's answer to the problem of the relation between God and the attributes would be to claim that God and the totality of attributes are identical, although they are conceptually distinct. Parchment's position regarding the problem of the essence of God would be to claim that God's essence is identical with both God and the totality of attributes, although they are all three conceptually distinct. Parchment does not discuss our third problem, the adequate conception of God by the human intellect. According to Spinoza, however, the adequate idea of an entity requires the idea of the essence of that entity. Hence, the adequate idea of God requires the idea of the essence of God. Further, we know that the idea of the essence of God is acquired via the attributes.[52] On the first interpretive option God, God's essence, and the totality of attributes are identical (although they are all conceptually distinct from one another). It seems, then, that one is conceiving the same "thing" whether one conceives God, God's essence, or the totality of attributes. The question, however, is whether the adequate idea of God, the essence of God, or the totality of attributes is acquired through any particular attribute or only through the totality of attributes. Since, according to Parchment, no *particular* attribute pertains to or constitutes the essence of God,[53] the conclusion might be drawn that, for Parchment, the human intellect must conceive the totality of attributes in order to have an adequate conception of the essence of God.

Critique of interpretive option one

There are several problems with the first interpretive option. One could question how Parchment could draw the conclusion that some X and Y can be both conceptually distinct and strictly identical. Parchment says that when X and Y are merely conceptually distinct there is only *one thing*. Parchment could be using this as a criterion of identity, resulting in the identity of God, God's essence, and the totality of attributes. However, Parchment wants to use Descartes' theory of distinction to support his view, and it is not good Cartesian usage to speak of an X and Y as being both conceptually distinct and strictly identical.[54]

There is a difficulty with Parchment's solution to the problem of the relation between God and the attributes on the first interpretive option. On this option God is identical with the totality of attributes. The problem with this interpretation of God and the attributes is similar to Hallett's problem of the indiscerptibility of the attributes in God.[55] That is, Parchment has not explained how God can be a totality of indiscrete attributes when the attributes are by nature distinct from one another.[56] Parchment's answer to the problem of the essence of God on this option would be to claim that the essence of God is identical with both God and the totality of attributes. This claim, it seems, is vulnerable to the same awkward question, i.e. what is a totality of indiscrete attributes? It seems that Parchment's answer to the third problem on this option would be to claim that a true conception of God would somehow involve the attributes (since the idea of the essence of God is acquired via the attributes). The question, then, would be whether the idea of the essence of God involves the idea of a particular attribute or the idea of the totality of attributes. Parchment does not say that the conception of a particular attribute can give rise to the idea of the essence of God. What he does say is: "What Spinoza cannot consistently claim is that thought alone (or any one attribute) pertains to or constitutes the essence of God".[57] Given this, one might think that Parchment would claim that the idea of the totality of attributes is necessary for the adequate conception of the essence of God (since God, the essence of God, and the totality of attributes are merely conceptually distinct on this interpretation, i.e. there is only one thing). The problem with this answer involves human conception. How is the human intellect to have an idea of the totality of attributes? Parchment has said that God's essence is indeterminate.[58] If God's essence is the totality of attributes and that totality is indeterminate, then the human intellect will be unable to conceive the essence of God. Whether there are only two attributes or an infinite quantity, it seems that the human intellect cannot have an idea of the totality of attributes, since the human intellect conceives the attributes only through themselves, i.e. the human intellect conceives the attributes as distinct from one another. Hence, the human intellect, it seems, cannot have an idea of a totality of indistinct attributes.

The three problems and interpretive option two

According to the second interpretive option, identity and distinctions of reason are mutually exclusive alternatives. So any X and Y are not identical if there is *any* distinction between them. On this interpretation of Parchment, there is no identity between God, God's essence, and the totality of attributes (since they are all conceptually distinct from one another).

On this option it seems that Parchment's answer to the problem of the relation between God and the attributes would be to claim that they are not identical; that is, God is not identical with any particular attribute, nor is God identical with the totality of indistinct attributes. This is because on Parchment's interpretation there is a modal distinction between God and the particular attributes, and a conceptual distinction between God and the totality of attributes. Parchment's answer regarding the problem of the essence of God would be to claim that the essence of God is not identical with God, nor is the essence of God identical with the totality of attributes (or any particular attribute). This is because on Parchment's interpretation the essence of God is conceptually distinct from both God and the totality of attributes. It seems that Parchment's answer to the third problem—that regarding the true conception of God—would be to claim that the conception of the essence of God is adequate for the true conception of God. On this interpretive option, the essence of God is not identical with either God or the totality of attributes. Hence, the true conception of God need not require the conception of the totality of attributes. Rather, the conception of the essence of God, by itself, would give rise to the adequate idea of God.

Critique of interpretive option two

The second interpretive option is troublesome, since it leaves unanswered both the problem of the relation between God and the attributes, and the problem of the essence of God. On this option God is not identical with the attributes. Hence we don't know what God is, since Parchment does not give a description of God apart from the attributes. Indeed, the same situation arises regarding the problem of the essence of God. We don't know what God's essence is, since on this interpretive option there is no description of the essence of God. That is, on option two we know that the essence of God is not identical with either God or the totality of attributes (or any particular attribute). We don't know, however, what the essence of God is.

Does option two pose any problems regarding the true conception of God? We know that the adequate idea of God requires the idea of the essence of God. Further, we know that the idea of the essence of God is acquired via the attributes. On the second interpretive option neither the totality of attributes nor any particular attribute is identical with the essence of God. Even so, Parchment claims that the conception of the totality of attributes gives rise to the conception of God. Indeed, Parchment says that 2d2 defines that which pertains to the essence of a thing as that which is merely conceptually distinct from the thing.[59] Further, he claims that the totality of attributes pertains to the essence of God.[60] Hence, for Parchment the totality of attributes is merely conceptually distinct from God. To say that whatever pertains to the essence of a thing necessarily involves the idea of the thing, and vice versa, does not entail identity between a thing and its essence. This reading of 2d2 is consistent with the second interpretive option. On this reading, when one conceives the totality of attributes, one conceives God. So, it seems that the idea of the totality of attributes (which is conceptually distinct from, and hence not identical with, the essence of God), gives rise to the idea of the essence of God (which is conceptually distinct from, and hence not identical with, God), which gives rise to the adequate idea of God.

This seems fine. The only sticking point is Parchment's understanding of the term "to pertain to the essence of". Parchment takes "pertains to the essence of" to mean "constitutes the essence of".[61] He says that the totality of attributes pertains to the essence of God. So, for Parchment, the totality of attributes constitutes the essence of God, whereas neither any one particular attribute nor the collection of the particular attributes pertains to or constitutes the essence of God.[62] Since the totality of attributes pertains to the essence of God, for Parchment the totality of attributes satisfies the stipulations of 2d2. So when one conceives the totality of attributes one conceives God.

Parchment claims that "to pertain to the essence of" in 2d2 means "to constitute the essence of". It is not clear, however, whether "constitutes the essence of" means "is identical with the essence of" on Parchment's view. If "constitutes the essence of" does mean "is identical with the essence of", then that which pertains to the essence of God is the totality of attributes, and the essence of God is the totality of attributes. On this reading, then, the totality of attributes is identical with the essence of God. This is problematic, since it conflicts with the second interpretive option, on which any X and Y are not identical if there is *any* distinction between them. The essence of God and the totality of attributes are conceptually distinct on the second option; hence, they cannot be identical. It seems, therefore, that if "to pertain to the essence of" means "is identical with the essence of" then Spinoza would have eliminated all discussion of "to pertain to the essence of" in 2d2 (since, on this reading, "pertains to the essence of" seems to add nothing to the definition). It seems reasonable, therefore, to conclude that that which pertains to the essence of a thing is not identical with the thing. This conclusion correlates with the second interpretive option.

But there is still the problem of the adequate conception of the essence of God on interpretive option two. For on this interpretation the totality of attributes is not identical with the essence of God. Parchment may still claim, however, that one must conceive the totality of attributes in order to conceive the essence of God. Indeed, this seems to be necessary, since according to Parchment the totality of attributes satisfies the stipulations of 2d2. So, when one conceives the totality of attributes (i.e. that which pertains to the essence of God) one conceives God.

The problem that remains on this interpretive option is the conception of the totality of attributes. I have claimed that the human intellect cannot conceive a totality of indistinct attributes, whether there are two attributes or an infinite quantity.[63] Perhaps Parchment can avoid this difficulty by claiming that the idea of a particular attribute gives rise to the idea of the totality of attributes, which gives rise to the idea of the essence of God. Parchment could do this by claiming that any particular attribute *pertains* to the totality of attributes. That is to say, he might claim that the idea of a particular attribute, gives rise to the idea of the *essence* of the totality of attributes which gives rise to the idea of the totality of attributes,[64] which gives rise to the idea of the essence of God. In this case one is not faced with the dilemma of the conception of a totality of indiscrete attributes. Instead, one may conceive the *essence* of the totality of attributes via any particular attribute. The problem with this view is that Spinoza makes no mention of this kind of hierarchy, i.e. particular attributes, the essence of the totality of attributes, the totality of attributes, the essence of God, and God. Spinoza speaks only of the particular attributes, the essence of God, and God.

What Parchment does say about the particular attributes is that they are "mode-like" relative to God and "substance-like" in relation to modes.[65] The particular attributes are not the essence of God on Parchment's interpretation, and no particular attribute pertains to the divine essence.[66] Indeed, Parchment says that "the divine essence is conceptually independent of its particular attributes".[67] It seems, then, that the idea of a particular attribute does not result in an adequate idea of the essence of God on Parchment's view. That is to say, for Parchment only the totality of attributes satisfies the stipulations of 2d2. So only the idea of the totality of attributes can give rise to the idea of the essence of God. Indeed, Parchment says that a particular attribute is perceived by the human intellect "as if" it constitutes the essence of God.[68] It seems, then, that the human intellect can have an adequate idea of the essence of God only by having an idea of the *totality* of attributes. Once again we are faced with the problem of the conception of a totality of indistinct attributes.

The totality as homogenized

On either interpretive option we are faced with the notion of "the totality of attributes". Parchment claims that the totality of attributes pertains to the essence of God (and that no individual attribute pertains to the essence of God). Thus, according to this view, the totality of attributes satisfies the stipulations of 2d2 relative to God. The notion of a totality of indiscrete attributes is a problem on either interpretive option. It is difficult to comprehend the nature or being of the totality of attributes; that is, what *is* a totality of indiscrete attributes? One way Parchment might deal with this problem is to argue that the totality of attributes is *homogenized*, such that there are no individual attributes in the totality. Then Parchment may claim that the essence of this homogenized totality is such that it may be conceived without conceiving the particular attributes.[69]

The question, however, is this: how can there exist a totality of indistinct attributes when the attributes are by nature really distinct from one another?[70] How do the attributes of thought and extension, for example, combine in such a way as to become indistinct from one another in the totality? Parchment might reply that although the particular attributes are by nature distinct from one another, God is an indivisible entity. Hence, the essence of God and that which pertains to the essence of God must be indivisible too. Since on Parchment's interpretation the totality of attributes pertains to the essence of God, the totality of attributes must be indivisible.

On a similar note one might say that the human body consists of cells that are homogenized in such a way that they are one holistic being. This seems unexceptionable, but one would not go so far as to say that the cells are homogenized to the point of not existing in the body as particulars. Indeed, it would be difficult to maintain the view that there are no discrete cells in the holistic entity, the human body. Similarly, what does it mean to say that the totality of attributes does not consist of particular attributes? What is this entity? It seems that the particular attributes *must* be elements of the totality of attributes. Simply to say (as Parchment does) that the totality of attributes is *logically prior* to the particular attributes does not seem to do enough to distinguish the notion of a totality of attributes from that of a collection of distinct attributes. In response to this, Parchment must claim either that the totality of attributes has no elements or that the elements of the totality are something other than the attributes. The second option seems untenable. The first leaves us with an entity whose nature is difficult to comprehend or explain. What is a totality of attributes that has no attributes as parts?

On the first interpretive option, the totality of attributes is identical with the essence of God. Hence, if the totality of attributes is the homogenized attributes, then the essence of God is the homogenized attributes.[71] It seems a mistake to view the essence of God as the totality of attributes. The essence of God must be a metaphysically possible entity; i.e. the essence of God cannot be an entity consisting of indistinct attributes since the attributes are by nature really distinct from one another. Further, the essence of God must be conceived via any particular attribute, since Spinoza spells this out in 2p1s.[72] So, the essence of God cannot be the totality of attributes, and the essence of God cannot be perceived through the totality of attributes.

Chapter 5

Benefits and Disadvantages of the Three Interpretations

Benefits and disadvantages of the "God is the thing that has attributes and modes as properties" interpretation

Bennett maintains that God is not the attributes; rather, God is that entity which *has* attributes and modes as properties. This interpretation has the advantage of avoiding the consequence that God is an entity that is *made up* of attributes, thereby avoiding the problems that arise from those views.[1] On Bennett's interpretation, the relation between God and the attributes is not a relation of identity, nor is the essence of God identical with the attributes. Rather, Bennett claims, the attributes are the way the intellect perceives God's essence.

On Bennett's interpretation the essence of God is the trans-attribute differentiae, i.e. the modes in abstraction from the attributes. One might claim that, on this view, it is impossible to have an adequate idea of the essence of God, since the intellect is incapable of conceiving the modes in abstraction from the attributes. While Bennett's view is unique and very interesting, it has the distinct disadvantage that the trans-attribute differentiae are not conceivable. However, this does not discourage Bennett; he claims that the human intellect has knowledge of the essence of God through the attributes. If the essence of God is the modes *in abstraction from* the attributes, then how is the human intellect to have an idea of the essence of God through the attributes? Bennett claims that the human intellect *can* have an idea of the essence of God, i.e. the trans-attribute differentiae, but only insofar as these modes are expressed through the attributes. According to Bennett, the essence of God is not the attributes, but is *expressed* through the attributes. Hence, the human intellect perceives the

Benefits and Disadvantages 55

essence of God via its expression through the attributes. So, the human intellect perceives the expression of the essence of God through any given attribute. Therefore, on Bennett's interpretation an attribute is perceived merely "as if" it constitutes the essence of God. It seems, then, that this is the closest the human intellect can get to the essence of God. Is this what Spinoza means by his claim in 2p47 that the human intellect has an adequate idea of the essence of God?

Benefits and disadvantages of the "God is the collection of attributes" interpretation

Curley claims that God is identical with the collection of distinct attributes. Donagan, it seems, also holds the view that God is the collection of distinct attributes. The claim that God is the collection of attributes has the advantage of accounting for all of the particular attributes (regardless of their number). In addition, this view seems to help explain Spinoza's apparent claims that God is the same thing as the attributes.[2] The claim that God is the collection of attributes also avoids the undesirable interpretation of the attributes as purely subjective in nature, since, on the "God is the collection of attributes" interpretation, the attributes exist in reality because they *are* God.

A disadvantage of this interpretation is that God appears to be a divisible entity; that is, God is an entity made up of really (and not merely conceptually) distinct attributes. Indeed, according to Spinoza's discussion in 1p10s the attributes are really distinct from one another; so the attributes are neither caused by one another nor conceived through one another. This, of course, means that the attributes are really distinct from one another; it does not mean that the attributes are really distinct from God. However, it is the claim that *the collection of particular attributes* is not distinct from God that is so difficult to explain.

It seems that on the "God is the collection of attributes" interpretation God is an entity that is composed of parts; that is, the particular attributes appear to be parts on this interpretation. In 1p12 and 1p13 Spinoza asserts the impossibility of the divisibility of absolutely infinite substance into parts:

> 1p12: No attribute of a substance can be truly conceived from which it follows that the substance can be divided.

> 1p13: A substance which is absolutely infinite is indivisible.

In 1p12 and 1p13 and their demonstrations Spinoza says that if substance is divided into parts, then the parts will either retain the nature of substance or they will not. If the parts do retain the nature of substance, then they will be infinite, self-caused, and different from one another in attribute. The qualities of being infinite, self-caused, and different from one another in attribute satisfy the definition of what it is to be a substance. The result is that from one substance many substances can be formed. Spinoza claims that this is absurd, since a substance is a self-caused entity, so no substance can be the cause of another substance. Therefore, a substance cannot be divided into parts that are themselves substances.

If, on the other hand, the parts into which a substance is divided do not retain the nature of substance, then the original substance would lose the nature of substance and, hence, cease to exist. That is, the substance would be a sum of parts of which none would possess the nature of substance. If none of the parts possesses the nature of substance, then the whole made up of the parts would not possess the nature of substance. This, too, is absurd since existence belongs to the very nature of a substance—and in this case no substance would exist. So substance cannot be divided into parts, whether those parts do or do not retain the nature of substance. If substance cannot be composed of parts, then there are no parts of a substance. The attributes cannot, therefore, be *parts* of God.

On the "God is the collection of attributes" interpretation, the attributes could be said to satisfy the stipulations of the first case in the demonstration of 1p12.[3] First, the particular attributes are *infinite* (in their own kind). Second, they are *self-caused;* that is, according to 1p10s the attributes are neither conceived through nor produced by one another.[4] Further, if the attributes *are* God (as Curley claims) then they must be self-caused. Finally, the attributes each *consist of a different attribute* (i.e. each attribute is of a different kind). So it seems that one could argue that, on the "God is the collection of attributes" interpretation, God is made up of parts which retain the nature of substance, viz. the particular attributes, and hence God is divisible, i.e. God is divisible into many substances. Those who hold the "God is the collection of attributes" view must explain how an entity made up of really (and not merely conceptually) distinct parts is nevertheless an indivisible entity.

Another disadvantage of the "God is the collection of attributes" position involves the understanding of the essence of God. In addition to claiming that God and the collection of attributes are identical, Curley maintains that the collection of attributes is *the* essence of God; yet Curley also says that each particular attribute is *an* essence of God. Donagan understands the essence of God to be the collection of attributes. This is the case because, according to Donagan, the collection of the attributes determines the being of God, and all of its kinds. So, Curley claims that both God and *the* essence of God are identical with the collection of attributes. However, Curley also says that God has an infinite number of essences, and that each attribute is *an* essence of God.[5] The result of this stance is that God's essence is both the collection of attributes and the particular attributes. This means that the essence of God is of two kinds, viz. the collective essence (the collection of attributes) and the individual essences (the particular attributes). This means that, on Curley's view, there is a sense (i.e. the collection of attributes or the collective essence sense) in which God and God's essence are *identical*, and there is a sense (i.e. the particular attributes or the individual essence sense) in which God and God's essence are *not identical*. These consequences seem undesirable since they complicate the notion of "the essence of God".

Donagan, it seems, claims that God is the collection of attributes and that the essence of God is the collection of attributes. Unlike Curley, however, Donagan does not think that the particular attributes are essences of God. Rather, Donagan claims that each attribute "pertains" to the essence of God, thereby avoiding the conclusion that there are "two kinds" of essences of God. Indeed, for Donagan, God has only one essence. According to Donagan no proper subset of the collection of attributes is the essence of God, but the full collection of attributes *is* the essence of God. One might claim that, on this view, each attribute is part of the essence of God. This certainly is a disadvantage, since on Donagan's interpretation God is identical with God's essence. Hence God's essence cannot have parts, since this would render God a divisible entity.

Another disadvantage of the view concerns the conception of God. One might claim that the human intellect must perceive all of the attributes in order to have an adequate idea of God since, on Curley's and Donagan's interpretation, God *is* the collection of particular attributes. Curley, however, thinks that the perception of at least one attribute is adequate for the perception of the essence of God. One single attribute is not, however, *the* essence of God. Rather one single attribute is *an* essence of God; for example, the attribute of extension is the essence of God only insofar as God is considered as extended. So, for Curley, having an adequate idea of God's essence does not necessarily entail the adequate idea of *the* essence of God, i.e. the collection of attributes. Indeed, according to Curley, the human intellect can have an adequate idea of God's essence by having an adequate idea of any particular attribute of God; that is, by having the adequate idea of *an* essence of God.

Donagan claims that the collection of particular attributes is the essence of God, that each particular attribute *pertains to* the essence of God, and that God is perceived through any particular attribute. This sounds much like Curley's view, since Curley, too, claims that although no attribute short of the full collection is *the* essence of God, the human intellect can nevertheless have an adequate idea of God's essence through any one particular attribute. No explanation is offered, however, of how the conception of one attribute can lead to the adequate idea of God when God is the collection of attributes.

Benefits and disadvantages of the "God is the totality of attributes" interpretation

Hallett maintains that the *distinction* of the attributes is *truly* conceived by the intellect. Nevertheless, Hallett says, "Substance as such suffers no such distinction."[6] Indeed, Hallett claims that God is identical with the indiscerptible attributes. A benefit of this claim is that it accounts for an infinite number of attributes while avoiding the problem of the divisibility of God. God on this view is the totality of all attributes; yet, in God the attributes cease to be distinguishable or separable from one another. A disadvantage of this interpretation is that it does not account for Spinoza's explicit claim in 1p10s that the attributes are really distinct from one another. That is, if the attributes are *really* (and not merely conceptually) *distinct* from one another, then, it seems, God cannot be the totality of *indistinct* attributes. This is a metaphysical impossibility. Another disadvantage of the "God is the indiscerptible attributes" interpretation is that, on this view, the distinction of the attributes appears to be relative to the intellect alone. Given this, one might claim that on this view the particular attributes are merely subjective in nature—an interpretation of the attributes that has been thoroughly rejected by contemporary commentators.

Hallett says that God is the totality of attributes and that, since there is no distinction of attributes *in* God, any particular attribute is the essence of God.[7] Hallett claims that it is the limitation of the human intellect that renders thought and extension discernible as distinct attributes; in God they are undivided. Indeed, Hallett says that, "as so united, *substantial* Thought is identical with *substantial* Extension, *substantial* X, etc."[8] This results in what appears to be the claim by Hallett that there is really only one attribute, and that attribute is God. A disadvantage of this view is that it does not adequately account for the particular attributes. Particular attributes must exist, since the intellect (which perceives the attributes truly) perceives them as really distinct from one another.

Whereas Hallett claims that God is adequately conceived through each particular attribute (although in God there is no distinction of attributes), Parchment, it seems, must claim that the essence of God is perceived through the totality of attributes. Parchment claims that in 2d2 Spinoza shows that a thing and that which pertains to the essence of the thing are conceptually distinct.[9] On Parchment's view the totality of attributes pertains to the essence of God. Hence one might think that, on Parchment's view, the totality of attributes and God are distinct from one another. However, Parchment also claims that God is identical with the totality of attributes.

Spinoza claims that the human intellect has an adequate idea of the essence of God because the human intellect has an adequate idea of that which gives knowledge of the essence of God, i.e. the attributes give knowledge of the essence of God.[10] It is a distinct disadvantage of this view that what is required for the adequate idea of God is the totality of attributes. It is impossible for the human intellect to have an idea of any attributes other than thought and extension. So, the adequate idea of the totality of indiscrete attributes cannot be the idea of the attributes of thought and extension *and* other attributes. The adequate idea of the totality of attributes must involve only the known attributes.

The human intellect must have an adequate idea of the totality of indiscrete attributes through the attributes of thought and extension. Indeed, the adequate idea of the totality of indiscrete attributes must arise from the idea of the known attributes whether the totality of attributes is the totality of two attributes or the totality of an infinite number of attributes. So, this view must require that the idea of either the attribute of extension or the attribute of thought must give rise to the adequate idea of the totality of indivisible attributes. Yet, according to Parchment, the particular attributes are not elements in the divine essence. Indeed, according to Parchment the particular attributes do not pertain to the essence of God; rather, the particular attributes are *effects* of the divine essence. 2d2 says that one cannot have an idea of a thing without simultaneously having an idea of that which pertains to the essence of the thing. Parchment says that the totality of attributes pertains to the essence of God. So, if one has an idea of the totality of attributes, then one has an idea of God. So it must be the case that, on Parchment's interpretation, the idea of an *effect* of God, e.g. the attribute of extension or thought, gives rise to the idea of the totality of attributes, i.e. that which pertains to the essence of God; this must be the case if the human intellect is to have an adequate idea of God.[11]

In 2p45–47 Spinoza says that the human mind has an adequate idea of the essence of God by having the idea of a *particular* attribute. However, on Parchment's interpretation particular attributes do not pertain to or constitute the essence of God. So it must be the case that, on Parchment's view, a particular attribute gives rise to the idea of the totality of attributes, which in turn gives rise to the idea of God.[12] Parchment does not explain how the idea of a particular attribute results in the idea of the totality of indiscrete attributes.

Chapter 6

Essences and True Ideas in Spinoza

In Chapter 1, I presented three problems involving God and the attributes in Spinoza's metaphysics. I have since examined three interpretive stances (including five commentators) relative to the three problems: the "God is the thing that has attributes and modes as properties" interpretation, held by Jonathan Bennett; the "God is the collection of attributes" interpretation, held by Edwin Curley and Alan Donagan; and the "God is the totality of attributes" interpretation, held by H. F. Hallett and Steven Parchment. I have shown that each of the interpretive stances has its benefits and disadvantages. In this chapter I will cover important topics in Spinoza that need to be understood before we can go on to discover the correct answers to the three problems. I will use what we discover in this chapter to arrive at solutions to the three problems in Chapter 7.

First, I will consider whether there is a difference (and if so, in what it consists) between something's pertaining to, constituting, expressing, and just being the essence of a thing. This process will naturally include a discussion of 2d2. Further, I will inquire into the nature of the relationship between things and their essences, and the relationship between a thing's essence and its power. I will also consider whether the attributes are finite or infinite in number. Once we have a clearer understanding of essences and their role in Spinoza's metaphysics, I will discuss the nature of adequate ideas for Spinoza, and the relation of adequacy to truth. Then I will discuss the difference between de dicto and de re conceptions. I will show that for Spinoza there are both de dicto and de re conceptions of the essence of God.

Essence and 2d2

Spinoza says that the human mind has an adequate idea of the essence of God.[1] What is it of which the human mind has an idea when it has the idea of the essence of God? What is the essence of God? Before we begin to discover what the essence of God is, we need to understand what Spinoza means when he uses the term "essence". The meaning of the term is the same for Spinoza whether one is speaking of the essence of a frog or the essence of God. 2d2 is a good place to start, since it is his purported definition of the term:

> 2d2: I say that to the essence of any thing belongs that which, being given, the thing is [NS: also] necessarily posited and which, being taken away, the thing is necessarily [NS: also] taken away; or that without which the thing can neither be nor be conceived, and which can neither be nor be conceived without the thing.[2]

The importance of this definition necessitates a careful and painstaking analysis. Here is what Spinoza says in 2d2. When that which pertains to the essence of a thing is given, the thing is given; and when that which pertains to the essence of a thing is taken away, the thing is taken away. Also, when the thing is given, that which pertains to the essence of the thing is given; and when the thing is taken away, that which pertains to the essence of the thing is taken away. The same applies to the conception of a thing. So, when that which pertains to the essence of a thing is conceived, the thing is conceived; and when that which pertains to the essence of a thing is not conceived, the thing is not conceived. Also, when the thing is conceived, that which pertains to the essence of the thing is conceived; and when the thing is not conceived, that which pertains to the essence of the thing is not conceived. Hence a thing's existence entails that which pertains to the thing's essence, and that which pertains to a thing's essence entails the thing's existence. In addition, the conception of a thing entails the conception of that which pertains to the essence of the thing, and the conception of that which pertains to the essence of a thing entails the conception of the thing.

Where does this leave us regarding the essence of God? When we apply 2d2 to the essence of God we get the following. When that which pertains to the essence of God is given, God is given; and when that which pertains to the essence of God is taken away, God is taken away. Also, when God is given, that which pertains to the essence of God is given; and when God is taken away, that which pertains to the essence of God is taken away. The same applies to the conception of God. So, when that which pertains to the essence of God is conceived, God is conceived; and when that which pertains to the essence of God is not conceived, God is not conceived. Also, when God is conceived, that which pertains to the essence of God is conceived; and when God is not conceived, that which pertains to the essence of God is not conceived. Hence God's existence entails that which pertains to God's essence, and that which pertains to God's essence entails God's existence. In addition, the conception of God entails the conception of that which pertains to God's essence, and the conception of that which pertains to God's essence entails the conception of God.

"To pertain to", "to constitute", and "to express" the essence of a thing

Notice that from 2d2 we can draw certain conclusions about "that which pertains to the essence" of a thing. It is not clear, however, that we can draw any conclusions from 2d2 about the role of the "essence" of a thing in Spinoza's metaphysics. That is, if "that which pertains to the essence" of a thing is simply the "essence" of the thing, then we can merely substitute "essence" for "that which pertains to the essence" in 2d2. In doing so we arrive at the conclusion that when the essence of a thing is given the thing is given, and when the thing is given the essence of the thing is given. Also, when the essence of a thing is taken away the thing is taken away, and when the thing is taken away the essence of the thing is taken away. We can draw the further conclusion that when the essence of a thing is conceived the thing is conceived, and when the thing is conceived the essence of the thing is conceived. Also, when the essence of a thing is not conceived the thing is not conceived, and when the thing is not conceived the essence of the thing is not conceived. Unfortunately, it is not clear that "that which pertains to the essence" of a thing in 2d2 simply means the "essence" of the thing. Indeed, it does not appear that Spinoza discusses the "essence" of a thing in this definition. We must therefore ask what Spinoza does discuss in 2d2; i.e. we must ask what it means for something to "pertain to" the essence of a thing.

Another locution in Spinoza's metaphysics that has been a cause of confusion and debate is the term "to constitute the essence of a thing". Some commentators take Spinoza's use of "constitute" to be synonymous with "pertains to" when Spinoza uses the term regarding the essences of things.[3] In addition to Spinoza's discussion of that which "pertains to" and that which "constitutes" the essence of a thing, he also refers to that which "expresses" the essence of a thing. Indeed, in Spinoza's definition of God he says that the attributes express the essence of God. Some commentators take Spinoza's use of "expresses" to be synonymous with "constitutes" when Spinoza uses the term regarding the essence of God.[4]

Are the terms "pertains to the essence of a thing", "constitutes the essence of a thing", and "expresses the essence of a thing" synonymous for Spinoza? If they are not, does the difference in meaning between the terms significantly affect the interpretation of God and the attributes in Spinoza's metaphysics? In order to discover answers to these questions, let's first consider what the five commentators think about Spinoza's use of these terms, and the impact of these terms on each commentator's view on God, God's essence and the attributes in Spinoza. I will first consider the locutions "constitutes the essence of a thing" and "pertains to the essence of a thing", and then follow with a discussion of "expresses the essence of a thing".

Bennett does not comment on Spinoza's discussion of "that which pertains to the essence of a thing"; rather, he takes 2d2 to be Spinoza's definition of "essence".[5] Bennett understands 2d2 to be a claim that the essence of a thing is that property which must be possessed by that particular thing and cannot be possessed by any other particular thing. According to Bennett, 2d2 defines the essence of a thing as "a qualitative necessary and sufficient condition" for a particular thing's being the thing that it is. For example, on this interpretation it seems that the qualitative necessary and sufficient condition for God's existence would be "having all the attributes and modes as properties".

In 1p10s Spinoza discusses the question of the identity between substance and attribute:

> 1p10s: From these propositions it is evident that although two attributes may be conceived to be really distinct (i.e., one may be conceived without the aid of the other), we still can not infer from that that they constitute two beings, *or* two different substances.

Bennett thinks that Spinoza does not identify a substance with its attributes, and for that reason he suggests that the term "constitute" in 1p10s should be understood not as something that implies identity, but as a verb that means "to fix", or "to define", or "to determine".[6] If Bennett interprets "constitute" in the same way relative to the discussion of the *essence* of a thing,[7] then if X constitutes the essence of Y, X is not identical with Y; rather, X fixes, defines, or determines the essence of Y. One might think that Bennett takes "pertains to" to mean "is identical with" (since he thinks that 2d2 is Spinoza's definition of the "essence" of a thing), and, since Bennett interprets the term "constitute" as something other than "is identical with", it seems that for Bennett "constitutes the essence of a thing" is not equivalent to "pertains to the essence of a thing".

Curley also says that Spinoza defines the term "essence" in 2d2.[8] So it appears that Curley also interprets "that which pertains to the essence of a thing" in 2d2 as equivalent to "the essence of a thing".[9] Hence, for Curley the "essence" of a thing is that which when it is given the thing is given, and when it is taken away the thing is taken away. On Curley's interpretation there are many essences of God. Indeed, for Curley each attribute is *an* essence of God, and the collection of attributes is *the* essence of God.[10] It is not clear, however, whether Curley takes 2d2 to be a definition of *an* essence of a thing, or *the* essence of a thing.[11] So we cannot know whether on Curley's interpretation *an* essence (i.e. an attribute) of God satisfies the stipulations of 2d2, or if only *the* essence (i.e. the collection of attributes) satisfies those stipulations.

Curley translates 2p10s2 in the following way:

> But I have said that what necessarily *constitutes* the essence of a thing is that which, if it is given, the thing is posited, and if it is taken away, the thing is taken away, i.e., the essence is what the thing can neither be nor be conceived without, and vice versa, what can neither be nor be conceived without the thing.[12]

In this passage Curley takes what necessarily constitutes the *essence* of a thing to be that without which the thing can neither be nor be conceived, etc. On this reading, then, what "constitutes" the essence of a thing is *the essence* of a thing (since Curley understands 2d2 to be the definition of the "essence" of a thing). So, it seems that, for Curley, "to constitute" the essence of a thing and "to pertain to" the essence of a thing are both synonymous with "is identical with" the essence of a thing.[13] Hence, for Curley, "constitutes the essence of a thing" is synonymous with "pertains to the essence of a thing".

Unlike Bennett and Curley, Donagan claims that 2d2 is a definition of "what pertains to an essence".[14] Further, Donagan thinks that each particular attribute pertains to the essence of God. For Donagan, if any particular attribute is given then God is given, and if any particular attribute is taken away then God is taken away. That is, according to Donagan, since each particular attribute expresses an infinite and eternal essence, each attribute is an attribute of God. So if some particular attribute were taken away then God would be taken away, since God (who is absolutely infinite) cannot lack any particular attribute. This is the case, according to Donagan, because if God were to lack some particular attribute then God would not be absolutely infinite; i.e. there would be some attribute that expresses an essence that does not belong to God's nature (and this is impossible according to 1d6).[15]

On this interpretation "pertains to the essence of a thing" does not mean "is identical with the essence of a thing" since, for Donagan, an attribute of a substance of more than one attribute cannot be identical with the essence of that substance.

Donagan says that, unlike the attributes of a multi-attribute substance, the attribute of a substance of only one attribute both "constitutes" and "is identical with" the essence of that substance.[16] On Donagan's interpretation, however, although an attribute of a substance of more than one attribute "constitutes" the essence of that substance, it is not the case that the attribute "is identical with" the essence of that substance. This is a puzzle, for in the case of a substance of one attribute the attribute constitutes, pertains to, and is identical with the substance, whereas, in the case of a multi-attribute substance each attribute constitutes and pertains to the essence of the substance, but no attribute is identical with the substance. It seems, then, that Donagan does view the terms "constitutes the essence of a thing" and "pertains to the essence of a thing" as synonymous. However, neither term can mean "is identical with the essence of a thing" when used in reference to God.[17]

Hallett does not comment on 2d2 in particular; so we cannot know whether Hallett takes 2d2 to be the definition of the "essence" of a thing, or the definition of "that which pertains to the essence" of a thing. Hallett does say that the attributes are the essence of God as apprehended truly by the intellect.[18] Hallett does not explain what "constitute" means for Spinoza, but he does claim that each particular attribute (and not the aggregate of attributes) constitutes the essence of God.[19] If Hallett holds the view that 2d2 is the definition of the "essence" of a thing, then since Hallett thinks that the attributes are the essence of God and that they constitute the essence of God, one might conclude that Hallett holds the view that "constitutes the essence of a thing" is synonymous with "pertains to the essence of a thing".[20]

Like Donagan, Parchment takes 2d2 to be the definition of "that which pertains to the essence" of a thing.[21] Further, Parchment claims that the totality of attributes pertains to the essence of God, and that the totality of attributes is conceptually distinct from God's essence. It is unclear, however, whether Parchment holds

Essences and True Ideas in Spinoza

the view that any X and Y that are conceptually distinct are also strictly identical. For that reason, we cannot know whether God's essence is identical with the totality of attributes on Parchment's view. Hence, we cannot know whether Parchment thinks "pertains to the essence of a thing" and "is identical with the essence of a thing" are synonymous.

Parchment clearly takes Spinoza's use of "constitute" to be synonymous with "pertains to" when Spinoza uses the terms in his discussion of the essences of things.[22] So whatever pertains to the essence of God constitutes the essence of God and whatever constitutes the essence of God pertains to the essence of God. According to Parchment, only the totality of indiscrete attributes pertains to (or constitutes) the essence of God. On his interpretation, however, the totality of attributes is conceptually distinct from the essence of God.[23] Once again, since it is unclear whether Parchment takes things that are conceptually distinct from one another to be identical with one another, it is impossible to know whether he believes that "constitutes the essence of a thing" means "is identical with the essence of a thing". So, we do know that Parchment thinks that "constitutes the essence of a thing" is synonymous with "pertains to the essence of a thing", but we do not know if these expressions are synonymous with "is identical with the essence of a thing".

There is not much discussion of the specific term "express the essence of a thing" in the literature on Spinoza. Donagan, however, is one commentator who does commit himself to an opinion on the subject. He says that it is the same relation to which Spinoza refers when he says that the attributes "constitute" or "express" the essence of God. However, Donagan says that Spinoza "tends to use 'express' when he particularly has in mind the kind to which the attribute assigns the substance, and 'constitute' when he has not".[24]

The locution "expresses an essence" appears first in Spinoza's definition of God. It also appears in 1p19d:

> Next, by God's attributes are to be understood what (by D4) expresses an essence of the Divine substance, i.e., what pertains to substance.

Here Spinoza refers to the attributes as that which "expresses" the essence of God; however, he cites 1d4 (in which he says that the attributes are that which the intellect perceives as "constituting" the essence of God). Spinoza appears to be drawing the conclusion that when something constitutes the essence of a thing, it also expresses the essence of the thing. Spinoza goes on in the same sentence (in 1p19d) to say that the attributes "pertain to" substance, i.e. God. Spinoza appears to draw the conclusion that, if the attributes express the essence of God, then they constitute and pertain to the essence of God. If this is true then, for Spinoza, the attributes express the essence of God because they constitute the divine essence, and the attributes pertain to the essence of God because they constitute and express the divine essence.

There are obviously conflicting opinions among commentators regarding the meaning of 2d2; some take 2d2 to be the definition of "the essence of a thing", while others think that 2d2 is the definition of "that which pertains to the essence of a thing". Further, even when commentators agree on what Spinoza is defining in 2d2, they disagree about what satisfies the stipulations of 2d2 relative to God. So, as far as we know, it may be that 2d2 is the definition of "the essence of a thing", or it may be the definition of "that which pertains to the essence of a thing". Further, it may be that the essence of a thing is identical with that which pertains to the essence of a thing, or that they are different from one another.

It appears that Spinoza may be using the terms "pertain to", "constitute", and "express" interchangeably. That is, it seems that whatever expresses the essence of a thing also constitutes the essence of the thing, and hence pertains to the essence of the thing. Indeed, in 1d6e Spinoza says that whatever expresses essence and does not involve negation pertains to the essence of God. The attributes express essence (by 1d6) and involve no negation (each attribute is perfect in its kind). Hence, the attributes pertain to the essence of God. So (by 1d6 and its explication) we know that what expresses the essence of God and does not involve negation also pertains to the essence of God.

Spinoza does appear to be referring to 2d2 in 2p10s2, yet he uses the term "constitute" in 2p10s2 where he uses the term "pertains to" in 2d2. Further, in 2p10 Spinoza seems to clarify his meaning of "pertain to the essence" with the phrase "constitutes the form". It seems reasonable, at this point, to assume that Spinoza does use the terms "constitutes the essence of a thing" and "pertains to the essence of a thing" interchangeably.

The essence of a thing

According to 2d2 "that which pertains to the essence" of a thing necessarily exists when the thing exists, and it is necessarily conceived when the thing is conceived; i.e. that which "pertains to" the essence of a thing is necessarily involved in both the existence and the conception (or idea) of the thing, and vice versa. One might think that if that which "pertains to" the essence of a thing is simply the "essence" of the thing, then Spinoza would have said so. Since Spinoza does not say so, we must consider the obvious possibility that that which pertains to the essence of a thing is not simply the essence of the thing. What might it be then?

One possibility is that that which "pertains to" the essence of a thing is something that gives rise to the idea of the essence of the thing, which, in turn, gives rise to the idea of the thing. So, in the case of God, for example, we have an idea of that which pertains to the essence of God. This gives rise to the idea of the essence of God, and the idea of the essence of God necessarily gives rise to the idea of God. On this view, each particular attribute may be said to pertain to the essence of God. That is, if a particular attribute is given, then God is given, and if a particular attribute is taken away, then God is taken away; if a particular attribute is conceived God is conceived, and if a particular attribute is not conceived God is not conceived. On this view an attribute is not the essence of God; rather, the idea of an attribute simply gives rise to the idea of the essence of God.

This interpretation of that which pertains to the essence of a thing seems very much like Curley's interpretation of God as an entity consisting of an infinite number of attributes. The attributes, according to Curley, are *essences* of God; i.e. each particular attribute is *an* essence of God, and the collection of attributes is *the* essence of God. On Curley's interpretation the idea of an attribute (i.e. *an* essence) is all that is necessary for the human intellect to have an adequate idea of *the* essence of God. There is a problem with this view, however; the problem involves the identity of God with the collection of attributes. In order to see the impact of this problem we need to consider what it is just *to be the essence* of a thing.

So far, we have considered Spinoza's use of the terms "pertains to" the essence of a thing, "constitutes" the essence of a thing, and "expresses" the essence of a thing. We have not yet discussed what it means for Spinoza simply *to be the essence* of a thing. Could it be that pertaining to, or constituting, or expressing the essence of a thing is just what it is *to be the essence* of the thing? We know that we can have an adequate idea of the essence of things, e.g. we have an adequate idea of the essence of God. However, since we do not yet know what it is *to be the essence* of a thing, we cannot, at this point, say what it is that we have an idea of when we have an idea of the essence of a thing.

A review of each commentator's stance on 2d2 relative to God is an appropriate place to start in the discussion of what it is *to be the essence* of a thing and what it is to be the essence of God. Bennett holds the "God is the thing that has attributes and modes as properties" view. Also, for Bennett, the 2d2 sense of the essence of a thing is the qualitative necessary and sufficient condition for the existence of the thing, or that *property* which is unique to the thing. So, for Bennett, the essence of a thing is a property possessed only by that thing. Hence, the essence of God would be the property of having the attributes and modes as properties. Being the thing that has attributes and modes as properties is not identical with the property of having the attributes and modes as properties. On this interpretation the essence of a thing is not identical with the thing.[25]

Curley and Donagan hold the "God is the collection of attributes" view. According to Curley, both God and the essence of God are identical with the collection of attributes. Hence, God is identical with God's essence. On this view the essence of a thing is identical with the thing. For Donagan, the essence of a thing determines the being of the thing and its kind(s). For Donagan, the attribute of a substance of only one attribute is identical with the essence of the substance, and the essence of the substance is identical with the substance; so, the substance is identical with the attribute. This is not the case, however, for a multi-attribute substance, since one attribute determines the being of that substance but not all of its kinds. Hence, the essence of God (a multi-attribute substance) is the collection of attributes, since the collection of attributes determines the being of God in all kinds. Also for Donagan, it seems that God is the collection of attributes. On this view the essence of a thing is identical with the thing.

Hallett and Parchment both hold the "God is the totality of attributes" view. Hallett claims that each attribute is the essence of God as truly apprehended by the intellect. However, according to Hallett, the attributes are indiscerptible in God; that is, God is the totality of indistinct attributes. No particular attribute can be identical with the totality of indistinct attributes. This means that no particular attribute can be identical with God. On this view, then, the essence of a thing is not identical with the thing. Parchment understands God and God's essence to be conceptually distinct from one another. It is not certain what Spinoza's God is for Parchment, but it is clear that on his view God's essence is the totality of indistinct attributes. However, whether Parchment thinks a conceptual distinction entails identity is unclear. On this view, we cannot know whether the essence of a thing is identical with the thing.

It seems, then, that there are two possible interpretations of what it is *to be the essence* of a thing. The essence of a thing may be identical with the thing or it may not be identical with the thing. Let us first consider the case in which a thing is identical with its essence. If the essence of a thing is identical with the thing, then Bennett's interpretation of God and God's essence cannot be correct. Bennett claims that God is *the thing that has the attributes and modes as properties*. Yet the 2d2 sense of the essence of God for Bennett is *having the attributes and modes as properties*. These two are not identical. On Bennett's view there is also *the source of the whole truth about God* sense of the essence of God. God's essence in this sense is the trans-attribute differentiae (i.e. the modes in abstraction from the attributes). The modes in abstraction from the attributes might be viewed as identical with the thing that has attributes and modes as properties (since these modes are the modes *under* the attributes). The problem with this view, however, is that Spinoza says that all modes are modes of attributes. Hence it is unlikely that God is identical with a system of modes *in abstraction* from the attributes.

If the essence of a thing is identical with the thing, then the "God is the collection of attributes" view does not seem plausible either. This is because of the divisibility problem. God is an indivisible entity; however, the attributes are really distinct from one another. To be really distinct entails both conceptual and ontological independence. So, since God is indivisible God cannot be identical with the collection of distinct attributes. So, if God's essence is the collection of attributes, then it seems that God cannot be identical with God's essence.

Finally, the "God is the totality of attributes" view does not seem to be correct in the case where a thing is identical with its essence. It seems that God simply cannot be identical with a totality of indiscrete attributes. This is because an entity that is a totality of indiscerptible attributes is an impossibility given Spinoza's conception of the attributes. They are really distinct from one another, and a real distinction entails separability—both conceptually and ontologically. So, if God's essence is the totality of indistinct attributes, then God cannot be identical with God's essence.

If, on the other hand, the essence of a thing is not identical with the thing, then God is not identical with God's essence. Bennett's interpretation of the essence of God includes two senses—the 2d2 sense (or the sense in which an essence of a thing is a qualitative necessary and sufficient condition for the existence of the thing), in which it seems that God's essence would be *having the attributes and modes as properties*, and the deeper sense (or the "source of the whole truth" sense) in which God's essence is *the trans-attribute differentiae*, which are the modes in abstraction from the attributes. Either sense of "the essence of God" is compatible with this reading of the essence of a thing. The problem with Bennett's view of the deeper sense of the essence of God, of course, is the unlikelihood that God's essence is the modes in abstraction from the attributes. The "God is the collection of attributes" view is not compatible with the interpretation of the essence of a thing as not identical with the thing, since on this view God is identical with God's essence (i.e. both are the collection of distinct attributes). The difficulty with the view is the problem of the divisibility of God. The "God is identical with the totality of attributes" view seems compatible with the understanding of the essence of a thing as not identical with the thing. On Hallett's view each particular attribute is God's essence and God is an entity in which the attributes are indiscerptible. However, we do not know whether on Parchment's interpretation the essence of God is identical with the totality of attributes or the essence of God is identical with God, because we do not know whether conceptual distinctions entail identity. The problem with the view is the ontological impossibility of God as an entity composed of indistinct attributes.

The relationship between a thing and its essence

All five commentators agree that the attributes pertain to the essence of God. Indeed, they would all agree that *all* the attributes pertain to the essence of God. Furthermore, Spinoza claims that the human intellect has an adequate idea of the essence of God. The human intellect, however, has ideas only of the attributes of thought and extension. This is not a problem since, according to 2p1s, we can have an adequate idea of God through one attribute. So it seems that one attribute is adequate for the conception of the essence of God.

When considering each of the three views of God in Spinoza's metaphysics, we find that the interpretation of the essence of God as *the trans-attribute differentiae*, i.e. the modes in abstraction from the attributes, does not seem promising, since Spinoza claims in 1p28d that all modes are affections of the attributes:

1p28d: For there is nothing except substance and its modes (by A1, D3, and D5) and modes (by P25C) are nothing but affections of God's attributes.

So it seems that there can be no modes in abstraction from the attributes. The interpretation of the essence of God as *the totality of attributes,* i.e. the indiscrete attributes, does not seem promising either, since Spinoza claims in 1p10s that the attributes are really distinct from one another. So it seems that there can be no totality of indistinct attributes. The most viable interpretation of the essence of God is *the collection of attributes view,* since Spinoza does say that the attributes pertain to the essence of God, and this view does not violate Spinoza's claim that the attributes are really distinct.

The collection of attributes view might be a reasonable interpretation if it were not for the problem of the divisibility of God. On this interpretation God is identical with the essence of God, and the essence of God is identical with the collection of particular attributes; hence God is identical with the collection of particular attributes. On this interpretation the essence of God is divisible; i.e. the essence of God is divisible into distinct attributes. If a thing and its essence are identical, then what is true of a thing must also be true of its essence. Hence the collection of attributes view raises a problem: if God is identical with the essence of God, then either the essence of God is not divisible or God is divisible. Neither of the two alternatives is possible. The attributes are really distinct from one another; hence, if the essence of God is the collection of attributes, then God's essence is divisible into distinct attributes; and according to Spinoza God is indivisible (by 1p12 and 1p13).

There are two alternatives regarding the essence of a thing: a thing may be identical with its essence or it may be different from it. Which alternative fits best with Spinoza's metaphysics? The first alternative—that the essence of a thing is identical with the thing—raises the problem of the divisibility of God on the collection of attributes view. For if the essence of God is the collection of attributes then God must be a divisible entity. This is impossible according to Spinoza. Spinoza does not, however, make any claims about the indivisibility of the *essence* of God. So, one might make the case that the essence of God is divisible and that the essence of God is identical with the collection of attributes. This, however, would mean that God cannot be identical with God's essence. Hence we should consider the second alternative—that a thing and its essence are not identical.

If a thing and its essence are not identical, then what is true of a thing need not be true of its essence. So on this interpretation of a thing and its essence, it may be that God is an indivisible entity whereas God's essence is divisible. The problem for the collection of attributes view is that God is identical with God's essence, i.e. the collection of particular attributes. If God is identical with God's essence, then what is true of God must be true of the essence of God. On this interpretation the essence of God cannot be divisible since that would require the divisibility of God.[26] However, even if we retain part of the collection of attributes view—that the essence of God is the collection of attributes—and consider that the essence of a thing need not be identical with the thing, we still do not have a complete view. If the essence of God is the collection of distinct attributes and a thing and its essence are not identical, then the question that remains regarding the relationship between a thing and its essence is: what is God? The challenge that remains, then, is to uncover an interpretation of God and the attributes wherein God is indivisible.

The relationship between a thing's essence and its power

What is a thing's essence? In 1p34 Spinoza says that God's power is God's essence:

> 1p34: God's power is his essence itself.

Is 1p34 the claim that a thing's power is identical with its essence? In 3p7d Spinoza identifies a thing's *power* or striving to persevere (i.e. the action of the thing insofar as it strives to endure or persist) with the actual *essence* of the thing:

> 3p7d: The power, *or* striving, by which it strives to persevere in its being, is nothing but the given, *or* actual, essence of the thing itself, q.e.d.

So, a thing's power is its actual essence. In using the term "actual essence" Spinoza is referring to the essence of a thing existing in space and time as opposed to a thing's essence as it exists in eternity.[27] An essence existing in eternity does not strive to persevere, since there is nothing that can overcome its presence in eternity. When the essence of a thing is instantiated in space and time the thing (and not the essence) must persevere in order to continue in existence, because there are things outside it that can hinder, impair, or halt its existence in actuality. In 3p7d Spinoza says that the power responsible for a thing's continuing existence is its essence. So, the essence or power of a thing is what allows it to persevere in actuality. Hence, we can say of a thing existing in actuality that its power is its essence, and whatever a thing actively does, it does through its essence. So it seems that, according to Spinoza, a thing's *power* is identical with its *essence*.[28]

We act according to our own essence or power. The activity of our essence or power is a striving, since there are things outside us that interfere with or impair our activity. The essence of a particular human being is a finite power. Since the essence or power of a human being is finite, the existence of each human being is limited in quality and time, according to its own essence or power. God acts according to God's own essence or power. Since there exists nothing outside God, there is nothing that can hinder God's power and activity. Whereas the essence of a human being is a finite power, God's essence is absolutely infinite and eternal power. Since God's essence or power is unlimited (i.e. absolutely infinite and eternal) there is nothing that can take away God's existence.

The number of attributes

We know by 1d6 that God's infinite and eternal essence or power is expressed through the attributes. How many ways is the essence or power of God expressed? That is: how many attributes are there? In 1d6 Spinoza appears to claim that there is an infinite number of attributes:

1d6: By God I understand a being absolutely infinite, i.e., a substance consisting of an infinity of attributes, of which each one expresses an eternal and infinite essence.

This definition, however, has also been interpreted in the following way:

By God I mean an absolutely infinite being; that is, a substance consisting of infinite attributes; each of which expresses eternal and infinite essence.[29]

This interpretation of 1d6 may be understood as meaning either that there is an infinite number of attributes, or that there is a finite number of attributes that are infinite in their own kind. It is essential, therefore, to include Spinoza's explication of 1d6:

1d6e: I say absolutely infinite, not infinite in its own kind, for if something is only infinite in its own kind; we can deny infinite attributes of it [NS: (i.e., we can conceive infinite attributes which do not pertain to its nature)]; but if something is absolutely infinite, whatever expresses essence and involves no negation pertains to its essence.

According to the explication, God is an *absolutely infinite* entity. Further, any expression of essence that involves no negation pertains to the nature of God. Each attribute expresses essence and involves no negation since it is infinite in its kind; therefore, every attribute expresses the essence of God.

Perhaps one might think that attributes finite in number are sufficient for the expression of the essence of God. This, however, is not what Spinoza says. Spinoza claims that if we conceive God not as an absolutely infinite entity, but as an entity that is infinite only in its own kind, then we can conceive attributes that do not pertain to the nature of God.[30] Spinoza goes on to say that if an entity is *absolutely infinite*, then any attribute that expresses essence and involves no negation pertains to the essence of that entity. God, by 1d6, is an absolutely infinite being; therefore every attribute pertains to the essence of God. It seems clear that the interpretation of 1d6 as meaning that there is a finite number of attributes, each of them infinite, is precisely what Spinoza strives diligently in the explication to avoid.

Still, one might claim that God as an entity of only two attributes does not violate the stipulation of 1d6e. That is, if two exhausts the number of attributes there are, then one might claim that two attributes *is* an infinity of attributes. On this view "infinite" just means: "all there can possibly be".[31] When we look carefully at what Spinoza says in 1d6e, however, it seems that it may not be plausible to interpret God as an entity of only two attributes. Spinoza says that if we understand God as an entity that is only infinite in its own kind—for example, an infinite extended thing—then we can conceive attributes that do not pertain to the nature of God.[32] It seems that if there are only two attributes, then Spinoza would have said that if we understand God as an entity that is infinite only in its own kind, then we can conceive *another attribute* which does not pertain to the essence of God. Spinoza seems to be referring to more than one other attribute in 1d6e—indeed, to an infinity of attributes.[33]

There is further support in Spinoza's text for the claim that God expresses essence via an infinite number of attributes. In the scholium to 1p10 Spinoza says:

> So it is far from absurd to attribute many attributes to one substance. Indeed, nothing in Nature is clearer than that each being must be conceived under some attribute, and the more reality, or being it has, the more it has attributes which express necessity, *or* eternity, and infinity. And consequently there is also nothing clearer than that a being absolutely infinite must be defined (as we taught in D6) as a being that consists of infinite attributes, each of which expresses a certain eternal and infinite essence.

Here Spinoza says that it is not absurd to attribute *many* attributes to one substance. "Many" usually means more than two. Further, if Spinoza is not referring to an infinite number of attributes, but rather to a finite number of attributes that are infinite in their kind, then his claim is redundant. That is, if one claims that there is a finite number of attributes, then, on this reading, "a being that consists of infinite attributes, each of which expresses a certain eternal and infinite essence" must mean that an attribute that is infinite is infinite in its own kind. This seems redundant, since an infinite attribute cannot be infinite in any other way than in its own kind. It seems unlikely that this is what Spinoza meant. Rather, Spinoza clarifies what he means by *absolutely infinite* in his definition of God.[34] Also, in 1p10s Spinoza asserts that since God is absolutely infinite, God has absolutely infinite reality or being, and that absolutely infinite reality or being necessarily expresses essence via an infinite number of attributes.

Adequate and true ideas

We now know that God's essence is identical with God's power. What is involved in having an adequate or true idea of the essence or power of God? In order to answer this question, we must understand what adequate and true ideas are for Spinoza.

Spinoza thinks that the relation of a true idea to its object is axiomatic:

1a6: A true idea must agree with its object.

Spinoza expounds on the nature of a true idea in 1p30d, where he claims it is self-evident that a true idea is an idea that agrees with something existing in nature.[35] Indeed, in 2p32d Spinoza says it is because all ideas in God agree with their objects that they are true ideas.[36] If, then, an intellect has an idea that agrees with some object existing in nature, that idea is a true idea; and if an intellect has an idea that does not agree with the object existing in nature of which it is the idea, then that idea is not a true idea.[37]

In 2p34 Spinoza says that an *adequate* idea in a human mind is a true idea.[38] In Letter 60 Spinoza explains the distinction between true and adequate ideas. Spinoza says that he recognizes only one difference between a true idea and an adequate idea, and that is that the word "true" refers to the extrinsic relation that a true idea has with its object, whereas the word "adequate" refers to the nature of the idea itself. An adequate idea, then, is a true idea considered without relation to its object. Spinoza defines an adequate idea in 2d4:

> By adequate idea I understand an idea which, insofar as it is considered in itself, without relation to an object, has all the properties, *or* intrinsic denominations of a true idea.

So an adequate idea has the internal characteristics of a true idea. What are these internal characteristics? Clearly it is not the agreement of the idea with its object, since that is an *extrinsic* relation. In 1p8s2 Spinoza says that a clear and distinct idea is a true idea.[39] Perhaps the properties of being clear and distinct are the intrinsic denominations of a true idea, i.e. perhaps an adequate idea is a clear and distinct idea.[40] Here is what Spinoza says in 2p29s:

> I say expressly that the Mind has, not an adequate, but only a confused [NS: and mutilated] knowledge, of itself, of its own Body, and of external bodies, so long as it perceives things from the common order of nature, i.e., so long as it is determined externally, from fortuitous encounters with things, to regard this or that, and not so long as it is determined internally, from the fact that it regards a number of things at once, to understand their agreements, differences, and oppositions. For so often as it is disposed internally, in this or another way, then it regards things clearly and distinctly.

So, it seems that an adequate idea is a *clear and distinct* idea; and a clear and distinct idea is an idea that is *internal* to a particular mind.[41] That is, a clear and distinct idea is not caused from outside the particular mind of which it is an idea. Indeed, in 2p43d Spinoza says that a true idea in a human mind is an idea that is adequate in God, insofar as God "is explained through the nature of the human Mind". In other words, an idea X, in a human mind A, is a true idea if and only if there is no cause of idea X outside A; hence, God does not have to go outside A in order to have idea X.

Therefore, a true idea X in mind A is an idea that is internal to A and has no causes outside A.

So, we can say the following about any true idea in any given human intellect: (1) it is an idea that agrees with its object (which necessarily exists in nature), (2) it is an adequate idea, i.e. it is a clear and distinct idea, and, hence, (3) it is an idea such that God does not have to go outside the human mind in order to have it. If an idea in a given human mind lacks any of these qualities, then that idea is not a true idea in that mind. We know, then, what it is for an idea to be true relative to the human intellect. The criteria for truth for ideas in God's mind (the infinite intellect), however, are not the same as the criteria for truth for ideas in the human intellect. Indeed, ideas that are false in a given human mind are always true in God's mind.

Michael Della Rocca discusses the claim by some commentators that, given Spinoza's thesis of parallelism, *every* idea must be a true idea.[42] According to 2p7 every idea has a parallel object. The claim, then, is that *every* idea is a true idea since every idea has a parallel object with which that idea completely agrees. Della Rocca, however, points out that 2p7c indicates that 2p7 is not about ideas relative to the human intellect; rather, the notion that ideas and objects are necessarily parallel is true relative only to God's intellect. Hence, Della Rocca claims that "For Spinoza, truth and falsity are mind-relative."[43] The mind-relativity of truth and falsity is the result of what Della Rocca calls "the containment thesis".[44] According to this thesis, all the individual ideas in the infinite universe constitute one individual mind, i.e. the infinite intellect (God's mind). All other minds, e.g. human minds, are *subsets* of the ideas that are contained within the infinite thinking thing. According to the containment thesis, then, every human mind is a part of God's mind. Hence, ideas that are in individual human minds are numerically one and the same with ideas that are in God's mind.

Given Spinoza's thesis of parallelism, then, all ideas in God's mind are true (since for every idea in the infinite intellect there is a parallel object with which the idea completely agrees). The human intellect, on the other hand, can lack ideas that are needed in order for a particular idea to be a true idea, i.e. a given human mind can lack necessary ideas that are outside that mind.[45] God's mind, of course, lacks no ideas (since the infinite intellect is the totality of all ideas). Hence on the containment thesis the content of an idea in a human mind is different from the content of the numerically identical idea in God's mind. That is, the content of a particular idea in a given human intellect may be incomplete, because the content of that idea may not include everything necessary for that idea to agree with the object of which it is an idea. For example, a particular human mind may lack a necessary idea that lies outside that intellect.[46] The content of that very same idea in God's mind, however, is necessarily complete, since the content of that idea includes everything necessary for that idea to agree completely with the object of which it is an idea. This is necessarily the case, since God's intellect includes every idea.

Whereas the infinite intellect has no inadequate ideas, it seems that most of the ideas in the human mind *are* inadequate ideas. Della Rocca explains what is missing in a given human mind when that human mind does not have an adequate idea, i.e. when that human mind has an inadequate idea. He says that 2p11c is Spinoza's explication of an adequate idea:

> From this it follows that the human Mind is a part of the infinite intellect of God. Therefore, when we say that the human Mind perceives this or that, we are saying nothing but that God, not insofar as he is infinite, but insofar as he is explained through the nature of the human Mind, *or* insofar as he constitutes the essence of the human Mind, has this or that idea; and when we say that God has this or that idea, not only insofar as he constitutes the nature of the human Mind, but insofar as he also has the idea of another thing together with the human Mind, then we say that the human Mind perceives the thing only partially, *or* inadequately.[47]

Earlier I said that a human mind could lack ideas (e.g. ideas that are outside that mind) that are needed in order for a particular idea to be a true idea. Della Rocca says that this is precisely what Spinoza claims in 2p11c. Hence, an idea in a given human mind is adequate if God has that same idea without having that idea in virtue of having an idea (or ideas) that lie outside that human mind. It follows, then, that an idea in a human mind is inadequate if God has the same idea in virtue of having one or more other ideas that are not ideas in that particular human mind.

What kind of idea is true, and yet inaccessible to the human intellect; that is, what kind of true idea lies outside the human intellect? Della Rocca shows that the causes of ideas can lie outside the human intellect.[48] Let's consider a particular idea, e.g. idea X (which has a mode of body B as its object) in human mind M. Recall that idea X in mind M is a true idea if and only if God does not have to go outside M in order to have idea X; so, idea X is a true idea in M if and only if there is nothing outside M that is part of idea X. Della Rocca shows that, given 2p9,[49] God has idea X in virtue of having the idea of the cause of idea X (i.e. the antecedent idea of X), and God has the idea of the antecedent idea of X in virtue of having the idea of the cause of the antecedent idea of X (i.e. the antecedent idea of the antecedent idea of idea X), and so on. We know, then, that each idea is caused by some previous idea. Here is where the problem of inadequate ideas arises for the human intellect. If any of the causes of idea X (i.e. the antecedent ideas of idea X) lie outside human mind M, then idea X is an inadequate idea in M. Recall that an adequate idea is an idea that has the intrinsic denominations of a true idea (i.e. an adequate idea is a clear and distinct idea). A clear and distinct idea is an idea that is internal to a particular mind. Hence, any idea whose causes lie outside the mind of which it is an idea is not a clear and distinct idea; hence, it is an inadequate idea. As Della Rocca says: "An idea is inadequate insofar as it is in a particular mind if that mind does not contain the ideas that are the causal antecedents of the idea in question."[50]

In 2p29s Spinoza explains the difference between an adequate and an inadequate idea. Spinoza says that an inadequate idea is determined externally and is the result of the mind perceiving things from the common order of nature, whereas an adequate idea is clear and distinct and is the result of the internal determination of the mind. Della Rocca has shown that the internal determination of a mind involves ideas that are caused only from inside that mind. On this account of adequate and true ideas we can see that most of the ideas in the human mind are inadequate, since most of the ideas in the human mind involve causes that lie outside it.[51] Absolutely every idea is in God's mind, however, and all ideas in God's mind are parallel to their objects. Hence, all ideas in God's mind are adequate and true ideas. Understanding what it is to have an adequate and true idea will help us understand what it is to have a true idea of the essence of God and, hence, a true idea of God.

De dicto/de re conceptions

A true idea of God or God's essence is different from a true idea of something said about God or God's essence. It is important to understand the distinction between these two kinds of ideas or conceptions. These two kinds of ideas or conceptions are de dicto and de re conceptions. When one conceives de dicto, one conceives a proposition; and when one conceives de re, one conceives a particular thing itself. Hence, the true conception of a thing itself is a de re conception. One can conceive the proposition: the essence of X is Y. This is an example of a de dicto conception since, in this case, one has conceived something that is said of X. If, on the other hand, one conceives X itself, then one has a de re conception since, in this case, one has conceived the thing itself.

There are both de dicto and de re conceptions relative to God. An example of a de dicto conception relative to God would be the conception of the proposition: God has an infinite number of attributes. The conceiving of this proposition is a de dicto conception, since it is the conception of something said of God. Indeed, the human intellect has no conception of any attributes other than thought and extension, so the conception that God has an infinite number of attributes is not the conception of *an infinite quantity of attributes* that God has; rather, it is a conception of *a proposition* said of God. If, on the other hand, one conceives God, then one has a de re conception since, in this case, one has conceived the thing itself.

How does one conceive a thing; that is to say, what is involved in the de re conception of a thing? According to Spinoza, to conceive a thing adequately one must conceive the essence of the thing. It seems, then, that for Spinoza the de re conception of a thing necessarily involves the conception of the essence of the thing. So the de re conception of God necessarily involves the conception of the essence of God.

According to Spinoza the attributes express the essence of God, and the human intellect perceives the attributes.[52] It follows that the human intellect has an idea of the essence of God. Indeed, in 2p45–47 Spinoza claims that the human intellect has an adequate idea of the essence of God, and that the human intellect has that idea via the attributes. According to 2d2, conceiving the essence of a thing results in the idea of the thing; hence, when the human intellect conceives the essence of God, the human intellect has a de re conception of God. The conception of the essence of God occurs through the known attributes; that is, the human intellect cannot conceive the essence of God through attributes unknown to the human mind. Hence, the human intellect has de re conceptions of God that occur through the known attributes. We must decide whether the de re conception of God is the result of the conception of one attribute, the collection of distinct attributes, or the totality of indiscrete attributes.

Summary and further considerations

We now know because of the stipulations of 2d2 that God's existence entails that which pertains to God's essence, and that which pertains to God's essence entails God's existence. Also, the conception of God entails the conception of that which pertains to God's essence, and the conception of that which pertains to God's essence entails the conception of God. In addition, we have found that it appears as though Spinoza may use the terms "pertains to the essence of a thing" and "constitutes the essence of a thing" interchangeably. The question that remains is: what pertains to the essence of God? We should consider whether the attributes pertain to the essence of God. If they do, then the question would be whether any given particular attribute, the collection of attributes, or the totality of attributes satisfies the conditions of 2d2 relative to God.

We also know that none of the three interpretations of God and the attributes is satisfactory on the view that a thing is identical with its essence. On this view what is true of a thing must be true for the essence of a thing. God cannot be identical with the trans-attribute differentiae. That is, God as the trans-attribute differentiae seems to be a metaphysically impossible entity, since Spinoza claims that all modes are modes of attributes. The collection of particular attributes cannot be identical with God because the collection of attributes is divisible into distinct attributes, and this would result in God being a divisible entity, too (which is impossible according to Spinoza). In addition, God cannot be identical with the totality of indiscrete attributes, since the attributes are really distinct from one another.

We have also considered the possibility that a thing is not identical with its essence. On this view, what is true of a thing need not be true of the essence of the thing. The interpretation of the essence of God as the trans-attribute differentiae does not seem to be a viable interpretation, because even though God need not fall under the same constraints as God's essence, the view itself has the seemingly serious problem of contradicting Spinoza's claim that all modes are modes of attributes. This seems to negate the possibility of the existence of modes that transcend the attributes. So, it does not appear possible that God's essence is the modes in abstraction from the attributes. Neither can the essence of God be the totality of indiscrete attributes, since the attributes are really distinct from one another. This leaves the collection of attributes as the most likely candidate for the title of the essence of God on the view that a thing and its essence are not identical. The interpretation of God's essence as the collection of attributes seems to be a viable interpretation since, if God is not identical with God's essence, then it may be the case that God is indivisible whereas God's essence is divisible. The challenge that remains on this interpretation of the essence of God is to discover what God is (since, on this interpretation, God is not identical with God's essence).

We also know that Spinoza identifies a thing's *power* or striving to persevere with the actual *essence* of the thing, and that the actual essence of a thing is the essence actualized in space and time. When the essence of a thing is instantiated in space and time the thing must persevere in order to continue in existence, and the power responsible for a thing's continuing existence is its essence. So, a thing's power is identical with its essence. Unlike the essences of modes, each of which is limited power, God's power is absolutely unlimited, and so God's essence is absolutely infinite and eternal power.

Whatever a thing actively does it does through its essence; and a thing is active insofar as whatever follows from the thing can be understood clearly and distinctly through that thing alone.[53] Absolutely everything follows from and is conceived through the attributes of God. So, once again there seems to be good reason to give careful consideration to the interpretation of the collection of attributes as the essence of God.

We have discussed the question of the number of attributes. Most commentators agree that Spinoza alludes to the existence of attributes other than thought and extension. Indeed, in the explication of 1d6 Spinoza seems to claim that there is an infinite quantity of attributes. An infinite number of attributes may not pose a problem for the interpretation of the essence of God as the collection of attributes. It does, of course, cause a problem for those who claim that the essence of God is the collection of attributes *and* that God is identical with God's essence, viz. the problem of the divisibility of God. So, it seems that we are on the right track to consider a thing as not identical with its essence.

According to Spinoza, a true idea agrees with its object and an adequate idea is a true idea. An adequate idea in a human mind is a clear and distinct idea; that is, it is an idea that God has without going outside that human mind (i.e. the idea is internal to that human mind). The human intellect has an adequate idea of the essence of God; hence, the idea of the essence of God is internal to the human mind. The question, then, is whether the adequate idea of the essence of God is the idea of the collection of attributes or something else; and, if the adequate idea of the essence of God is the idea of the collection of attributes, whether that idea is the idea of an *infinite* collection of attributes.

This question may be elucidated by considering the difference between de dicto and de re conceptions. A de dicto conception is the conception of something said of a thing; i.e. it is a conception of a *proposition*. A de re conception, on the other hand, is a conception of a *thing itself*. In Chapter 7, I will show that the answer to the question of the adequate idea of the essence of God is found in the distinction between de dicto and de re conceptions.

Chapter 7

The Essence of Spinoza's God

In Chapter 1, I said that there are three main problems regarding God and the attributes in Spinoza's metaphysics: (1) the problem of the relation of God to the attributes, (2) the problem of the essence of God, and (3) the problem of the true conception of God. These problems translate into three questions: (1) What is the relation between God and the attributes? (2) What is the essence of God? (3) What is a true conception of God?[1] The first step required in order to find satisfactory answers to these questions is to consider the views held by commentators regarding God and the attributes in Spinoza. I presented and examined three interpretations of God and the attributes, from five commentators, and considered the answers to the three problems according to each commentator's view. I then considered the benefits and disadvantages of each view. I also discussed various important notions in Spinoza's metaphysics that are critical to the topic at hand. Now, in this chapter, I will suggest an interpretation of God and the attributes that is motivated by Spinoza's claim in 1p34 that God's power is God's essence. This interpretation takes 2d2 to be crucial in understanding Spinoza's stance on the essence of God. The interpretation of God and the attributes I will propose avoids the problem of the divisibility of God and takes into account all the attributes regardless of their number. The interpretation of God and the attributes I will suggest will involve the claim that a de re conception of God follows from an adequate idea of the essence of God. I will invoke Michael Della Rocca's account of the opacity of attribute contexts in order to support my view of de re conceptions of God. I will explain what the attributes *are* for Spinoza and the *role* the attributes play in his understanding of reality. I will show that by viewing the attributes through this alternative interpretation many of the problems incurred by other interpretations can be solved or avoided altogether. Indeed, I will resolve the three problems posed in Chapter 1.

In my interpretation of God and the attributes I concur with Steven Parchment's initial approach to the problem. That is, I agree with Parchment's emphasis on 2d2 in his consideration of the relation between God and the attributes. I also take into account Bennett's suggestion that to read 2d2 as a claim that the essence of X is X renders the definition vacuous. I agree with Curley and Donagan that the attributes are really distinct from one another and that the distinct attributes are involved in the conception of God. Also, I suggest that the most useful aspect of Hallett's view is not his interpretation of the attributes as indiscerptible in God (a view that Parchment seems to espouse), but rather his emphasis on Spinoza's God as the maximally active entity. In 2d2 Spinoza explains the relation between a thing and its essence. According to the stipulations set out in 2d2, there is both an ontological and conceptual dependence between a thing and that which pertains to the essence of the thing; so there is both an ontological and conceptual dependence between God and that which pertains to God's essence. This means both that God's existence entails that which pertains to God's essence and that which pertains to God's essence entails God's existence, and that every true idea of God entails a true idea of that which pertains to God's essence and every true idea of that which pertains to God's essence entails a true idea of God. I will show that clearly understanding Spinoza's meaning in 2d2 leads to a plausible interpretation of the attributes of God.

In Chapter 6, I suggested that we consider God not to be identical with God's essence (since none of the three interpretations of God and the attributes works on the view that a thing is identical with its essence). Also, I suggested that we consider whether the attributes pertain to the essence of God. We must decide, then, whether it is any given particular attribute, the collection of distinct attributes, or the totality of indistinct attributes which pertains to the essence of God. In addition to asking whether the attributes pertain to the essence of God, we must ask whether that which pertains to the essence of God *is* the essence of God. Hence, we must ask whether there is a distinction between *that which pertains to the essence* of God and *the essence* of God. So if we find that the attributes pertain to the essence of God, then we will need to know whether the attributes *are* the essence of God or whether the attributes are just *related to* the essence of God in some way.

If that which pertains to the essence of God is not the essence of God, then we need to discover what the essence of God is and what the attributes are relative to the essence of God. If that which pertains to the essence of God *is* the essence of God, and if the attributes pertain to the essence of God, then we need to know whether the adequate idea of the essence of God is the idea of any given particular attribute, the idea of the collection of attributes, or the idea of the totality of attributes. Further, if the adequate idea of the essence of God is the idea of the collection of attributes, then we must ask whether that idea is the idea of an *infinite* collection of attributes. Since the human intellect has an adequate (and hence true) idea of the essence of God, the adequate idea of the essence of God is internal to the human mind. We must, then, ask whether the human mind can have an adequate idea of the essence of God if the essence of God is the collection of an infinite number of attributes.

In order to understand what the essence of God is I will show that, for Spinoza, the essence of a thing is given by the definition of the thing (i.e. the definition of the thing is the statement of the essence of the thing). I will then discuss the definition of Spinoza's God (1d6) and ask whether that definition correlates with his claim in 1p34 that God's power is God's essence. I will argue that neither God nor God's essence is identical with the attributes. I will suggest instead that God is an absolutely infinite and eternal being that has infinite attributes, that God's essence is absolutely infinite and eternal power, and that the essence of God is what is constituted and expressed by each of the infinite attributes. I will consider the distinction between de dicto and de re conceptions, and I will conclude that the conception of the essence of God through its expression via a given particular attribute results in the de re idea of God.

The essence of God and 2d2

In order to understand what the essence of God is, we should start by reviewing 2d2 and consider 2d2 when applied to God. Then we may consider whether the attributes satisfy the stipulations of 2d2 relative to God. In 2d2 Spinoza says that when that which pertains to the essence of a thing is given, the thing is given; and when that which pertains to the essence of a thing is taken away, the thing is taken away. Also, when the thing is given, that which pertains to the essence of the thing is given; and when the thing is taken away, that which pertains to the essence of the thing is taken away. The same applies to the conception of a thing. So, when that which pertains to the essence of a thing is conceived, the thing is conceived; and when that which pertains to the essence of a thing is not conceived, the thing is not conceived. Also, when the thing is conceived, that which pertains to the essence of the thing is conceived; and when the thing is not conceived, that which pertains to the essence of the thing is not conceived. Hence a thing's existence entails that which pertains to the thing's essence, and that which pertains to a thing's essence entails the thing's existence. In addition, the conception of a thing entails the conception of that which pertains to the essence of the thing, and the conception of that which pertains to the essence of a thing entails the conception of the thing.

According to 2d2, then, when that which pertains to the essence of God is given, God is given; and when that which pertains to the essence of God is taken away, God is taken away. Also, when God is given, that which pertains to the essence of God is given; and when God is taken away, that which pertains to the essence of God is taken away. The same applies to the conception of God. So, when that which pertains to the essence of God is conceived, God is conceived; and when that which pertains to the essence of God is not conceived, God is not conceived. Also, when God is conceived, that which pertains to the essence of God is conceived; and when God is not conceived, that which pertains to the essence of God is not conceived. Hence God's existence entails that which pertains to God's essence, and that which pertains to God's essence entails

God's existence. In addition, the conception of God entails the conception of that which pertains to God's essence, and the conception of that which pertains to God's essence entails the conception of God.

Most commentators agree that the attributes pertain to the essence of God. We know that there are at least two attributes (and possibly more). If the *particular* attributes pertain to the essence of God, then when the attribute of thought is given, God is given; and when the attribute of thought is taken away, God is taken away. Also, when God is given, the attribute of thought is given; and when God is taken away, the attribute of thought is taken away. Further, if the attribute of thought pertains to the essence of God, then when the attribute of thought is conceived, God is conceived; and when the attribute of thought is not conceived, God is not conceived. Also, when God is conceived, the attribute of thought is conceived; and when God is not conceived, the attribute of thought is not conceived. On this reading of 2d2 the attribute of extension also pertains to the essence of God. So, when the attribute of extension is given, God is given; and when the attribute of extension is taken away, God is taken away. Also, when God is given, the attribute of extension is given; and when God is taken away, then the attribute of extension is taken away. Once again one can draw the further conclusion that if the attribute of extension pertains to the essence of God, then when the attribute of extension is conceived, God is conceived; and when the attribute of extension is not conceived, God is not conceived. Also, when God is conceived, the attribute of extension is conceived; and when God is not conceived, the attribute of extension is not conceived.

This, however, does not seem to satisfy the stipulation of 2d2. 2d2 claims that whatever pertains to the essence of a thing is that without which the thing cannot be conceived. If the particular attributes are that which pertains to the essence of God, then each attribute is sufficient but not necessary for the conception of God.[2] The claim that each *particular* attribute pertains to the essence of God seems to be prima facie ruled out by 2d2, since that which pertains to the essence of a thing is *necessary* for the conception of the thing. So, if each of the particular attributes pertains to the essence of God, then it cannot be the case that when just one of them is conceived, God is conceived. In other words, if the particular attributes pertain to the essence of God, then *all of the particular attributes* must be conceived when God is conceived; and when God is conceived *all of the particular attributes* must be conceived (since that which pertains to the essence of God is necessary for the conception of God, and vice versa). *All of the particular attributes* are, of course, either the *collection* of particular attributes or the *totality* of indistinct attributes. However, the *collection* of particular attributes cannot be that without which God cannot be conceived, since Spinoza says that we can conceive an infinite being through one attribute alone.[3] Also, the *totality* of indistinct attributes cannot be that without which God cannot be conceived, since the human intellect cannot conceive a totality of indiscrete attributes. If neither the *particular* attributes nor the *collection* or *totality* of attributes pertains to the essence of God, then what fulfills the stipulations of 2d2 relative to God? What pertains to the essence of God?

One might suggest that if that which pertains to the essence of a thing is simply the essence of the thing, then Spinoza would have made that explicit. Spinoza does not appear to make this claim. Indeed, there are commentators who claim that 2d2 is not the definition of the essence of a thing. How can the human intellect have an adequate idea of the essence of God if the particular attributes are not that which pertains to the essence of God? Also, what is that which pertains to the essence of God if it is not just the essence of God? Bennett thinks that the attributes pertain to the essence of God, and that the essence of God is the trans-attribute differentiae (i.e. the modes in abstraction from the attributes). On this view that which pertains to the essence of God is not identical with the essence of God. Curley and Donagan think the attributes pertain to the essence of God. On the "God is the collection of attributes" view the collection of attributes is the essence of God. Curley, however, goes further in claiming that each particular attribute is *an* essence of God. So, for Curley, God has many essences; that is, God has one essence per attribute plus the essence that is the collection of all the attributes. On this view that which pertains to the essence of God is not identical with the essence of God.[4] Hallett thinks there is no distinction of attributes in substance, and Parchment thinks that the totality of attributes pertains to the essence of God. On the "God is the totality of attributes" view the totality of indiscrete attributes is the essence of God. On this view there is only one essence of God and it may be identical with that which pertains to the essence of God.[5] Each of these interpretations of the essence of God and that which pertains to the essence of God has its benefits and its disadvantages.[6]

Della Rocca, on the other hand, presents a very different interpretation of the attributes of God, a view that comports with what Spinoza says in 2d2. According to Della Rocca, parallelism in Spinoza's metaphysics is simply a thesis regarding two separate ways of understanding the causal chain of reality.[7] Della Rocca says:

> The duality in Spinoza's parallelism is not one between distinct things but between distinct descriptions or ways of conceiving things. Thus we might say that Spinoza's parallelism is not ontological but semantical in character.[8]

On Della Rocca's view, a mode under the attribute of thought really is one and the same thing as that mode under the attribute of extension; they are numerically identical. That is, for Della Rocca, there are no parallel *modes*. This is because, on Della Rocca's interpretation, attribute contexts are opaque. Hence, there are no actually existing parallel modes; rather, there are simply parallel ways of *conceiving* or *describing* modes.[9] Take, for example, mode A. According to Della Rocca, there exists no extended mode A that is ontologically distinct from thinking mode A. Rather, there is a single mode A and there are parallel ways of conceiving or describing mode A; so, A can be conceived or described insofar as it is a thinking thing, and A can be conceived or described insofar as it is an extended thing. On Della Rocca's account, then, a mode under the attribute of thought really is one and the same thing as that mode under the attribute of extension. There are, then, parallel ways of conceiving or describing things. That is, a thing can be conceived or described insofar as it is conceived or described as a thinking thing or as an extended thing, etc.

On Della Rocca's interpretation, the attributes really exist and they are really distinct.[10] Indeed, the attributes are distinct ways in which modes are conceived *and* they are distinct ways in which the essence of God is conceived. On Della Rocca's interpretation of the attributes of God the attributes do constitute the essence of God; each constitutes the essence of God insofar as the essence of God is conceived or described in a particular way.[11] This aspect of Della Rocca's interpretation is precisely why his view comports with 2d2.[12] In Chapter 6, I showed that Spinoza appears to use the terms "constitutes the essence of a thing" and "pertains to the essence of a thing" interchangeably. Hence, on Della Rocca's interpretation, since each attribute constitutes the essence of God each attribute pertains to the essence of God—which is to say that each attribute satisfies the stipulations of 2d2. The attribute of thought, for example, satisfies the stipulations of 2d2 insofar as God is described as an infinite thinking substance, and the attribute of extension satisfies the stipulations of 2d2 insofar as God is described as an infinite extended substance. So, when a particular attribute is given, God (insofar as God is understood or described in that particular way) is given; and when that particular attribute is taken away, God (insofar as God is understood or described in that particular way) is taken away. Further, when God (insofar as God is understood or described in a particular way) is given, that particular attribute is given; and when God (insofar as God is understood or described in a particular way) is taken away, that particular attribute is taken away.

Earlier in this section, I showed that a problem arises on the view that the particular attributes satisfy the stipulations of 2d2 relative to God. I said that the problem is that on this view each attribute is sufficient but not necessary for the conception of God, and that this seems impossible, since according to 2d2 that which pertains to the essence of a thing is *necessary* for the conception of the thing. If that which pertains to the essence of a thing is *necessary* for the conception of the thing, then on the view that the particular attributes satisfy the stipulations of 2d2 relative to God, when the attribute of thought is conceived, God is conceived, and when the attribute of thought is not conceived, God is *not* conceived. The same would be the case for any other attribute. However, those who hold the view that the particular attributes satisfy the stipulations of 2d2 relative to God generally want to claim that God may be conceived through any particular attribute alone. But we cannot have it both ways. That which pertains to the essence of a thing is either necessary for the conception of the thing or it is not. If that which pertains to the essence of a thing is necessary for the conception of the thing, then on the view that the particular attributes pertain to the essence of God, the conception of all the particular attributes (and not just any attribute) must be necessary for the conception of God. So, it seems that if the particular attributes pertain to the essence of God, then it cannot be the case that when just one of them is conceived, God is conceived. Della Rocca avoids this problem with his view of the opacity of attribute contexts. On his interpretation all of the attributes satisfy the stipulations of 2d2. Hence it is not the case that when the attribute of thought is not conceived, God is not conceived, or that when God is conceived, the attribute of thought is conceived. On Della Rocca's interpretation the attributes are different ways of conceiving or describing the essence of God. So, if the attribute of thought is not conceived, God may still be conceived; that is, God may be conceived in another way—for example, God may be conceived insofar as God is the infinite extended substance. Also, when God is conceived the attribute of extension may not be conceived, i.e. God may be conceived in another way: for example, God may be conceived insofar as God is the infinite thinking substance.

So, some particular attribute is conceived when God is conceived, and when some particular attribute is not conceived God can still be conceived, i.e. God can be conceived through another attribute. Hence, on Della Rocca's interpretation, 2d2 does not stipulate either that certain particular attributes pertain to the essence of God, or that only the collection of attributes pertains to the essence of God. Rather, for Della Rocca 2d2 allows the claim that any particular attribute pertains to the essence of God. This gives us a good start to understanding what the essence of God is in Spinoza's metaphysics.

God and de dicto/de re conceptions

In Chapter 6, I discussed the difference between de dicto and de re conceptions. In addition to understanding Spinoza's meaning in 2d2, understanding the distinction between de dicto and de re conceptions (or ideas) is critical to uncovering the answers to the three questions about God and the attributes in Spinoza's metaphysics. A de dicto conception is the conception of something said of a thing, whereas a de re conception is the conception of a thing itself. I suggested, therefore, that the true conception of a thing itself is a de re conception. For Spinoza there are both de dicto and de re conceptions relative to God. An example of a de dicto conception relative to God would be the conception of the proposition: God has an infinity of attributes. This is a de dicto conception, since the human intellect has no knowledge of or direct connection with any attributes other than thought and extension. Hence, the conception that God has an infinity of attributes is not the conception of *an infinity of attributes* that God has; rather, it is a conception of *a proposition* said of God. If, on the other hand, one conceives God, then one has a de re conception, since in this case one has conceived the thing itself. How does the human intellect have a de re conception of God?

According to Spinoza the attributes express the essence of God, and the human intellect perceives the attributes.[13] It follows that the human intellect has an idea of the essence of God. Indeed, Spinoza claims that the human intellect has an adequate idea of the essence of God, and that the human intellect has that idea via the attributes.[14] For Spinoza, the idea of the essence of a thing results in the idea of the thing.[15] The human intellect has an adequate idea of the essence of God via the known attributes, viz. the attributes of thought and extension. Hence, the human intellect has a de re conception of God. The question that remains, then, is whether the de re conception of God is the result of the conception of one attribute, the conception of the collection of distinct attributes, or the conception of the totality of indiscrete attributes.

On Bennett's "God is the thing that has attributes and modes as properties" interpretation, no particular attribute, nor the collection of particular attributes, nor the totality of indistinct attributes is the essence of God; rather, the essence of God is the trans-attribute differentiae (the modes in abstraction from the attributes). Further, according to Bennett the human intellect cannot conceive the essence of God directly, since the human intellect cannot have an idea of the modes in abstraction from the attributes; instead, the human intellect perceives the essence of God by comprehending the trans-attribute differentiae expressed as thinking and as extended. That is, since the human intellect cannot have an idea of the modes in abstraction from the attributes, the human intellect perceives the trans-attribute differentiae (the essence of God) via the attributes through which they are expressed. So, it seems that on this interpretation the human intellect can never have a de re conception of God, since to have a de re conception of God the human intellect must have an adequate idea of the essence of God (and the human intellect cannot have an idea of the trans-attribute differentiae).[16]

De re conceptions of God by the human intellect involve only the known attributes. This results in certain problems for those commentators who hold the view that God's essence is the collection of attributes and that God is identical with God's essence. The human intellect has ideas only of the attributes of thought and extension. If the essence of God is the collection of attributes and there exist attributes other than thought and extension, then the human intellect cannot have an adequate idea of the essence of God. That is, no other attributes can be conceived by the human intellect, since no attribute can be conceived through another.[17] The adequate idea of the essence of a thing is necessary for the de re conception of a thing. Hence, on this interpretation, the human intellect cannot have a de re conception of God, since the human intellect cannot have an adequate idea of the collection of attributes (the essence of God).[18]

One who holds the view that God is identical with the collection of attributes might want to claim that a de re conception (or idea) of God follows from a de dicto conception (or idea). As I mentioned earlier, one might claim that the de re conception of God follows from the conception of the proposition: God has an infinity of attributes. However, remember that the conception that God has an infinity of attributes is not the conception of the attributes themselves; rather, it is a conception of a *proposition* said of God—a conception of something said about God. Further, it is not possible for the human intellect to have a de re conception of an infinity of attributes, since the human intellect has no direct connection with any attributes other than thought and extension. It seems impossible, then, that a de re conception of an infinity of attributes can be the result of a de dicto conception.[19]

Other commentators hold the view that the essence of God is the totality of attributes.[20] The claim that the totality is indiscerptible does not hold, since the particular attributes must be elements of the totality. That is, the particular attributes must be elements of the totality since the intellect conceives the attributes truly, *and* the intellect conceives the attributes as *really distinct* from one another.[21] So, the attributes are really distinct from one another and hence it is impossible that they exist indivisibly in God. This means that the intellect cannot conceive the attributes as an indivisible totality. There is a problem with this interpretation of the essence of God whether or not God is thought to be identical with God's essence. The de re conception of a thing requires the adequate idea of the essence of a thing. The human intellect cannot have an adequate idea of the essence of God on this view (since the attributes cannot be conceived as an indiscerptible totality). Since a de re conception of a thing is dependent on the conception of the essence of the thing—and on this interpretation of the essence of God the human intellect cannot have an idea of God's essence—the human intellect cannot have a de re conception of God.

It seems that the human intellect cannot have an adequate idea of the essence of God on any of the three interpretations of God and the attributes. The human intellect cannot conceive the trans-attribute differentiae, or the collection of attributes (if indeed there is an infinity of attributes),[22] or the totality of indiscrete attributes. What, then, is the adequate idea of the essence of God for the human intellect?

The essence of God

In order to answer this question regarding the essence of God, we need to discover the relationship between the attributes and that which pertains to the essence of God, and the relationship between that which pertains to the essence of God and the essence of God. Della Rocca offers a promising account of the attributes of God, since his account seems to comport with three important definitions in Spinoza's metaphysics: the definition of the attributes (1d4), the definition of God (1d6), and the definition of "that which pertains to the essence of a thing" (2d2).

On Della Rocca's understanding, there is more than one way to view the essence of God: there are the first- and second-order essences of God. According to Della Rocca, the essence of God consists in "being the substance of infinite attributes" when God is *described* as God simpliciter (i.e. when God is described as "the substance of infinitely many attributes").[23] This is the essence of God under the description "God". Della Rocca calls this the second-order essence of God, since the essence of God under the description "God" refers to God's essence under all of the other descriptions of God—God described as the thinking substance, God described as the extended substance, etc. The definition of a thing is the statement of the essence of the thing.[24] Hence, according to Della Rocca, 1d6 is the definition of God (i.e. the statement of the essence of God) as God simpliciter. So, 1d6 is the statement of the second-order essence of God.

Just as attribute contexts are referentially opaque according to Della Rocca's account of the modes of God, attribute contexts are referentially opaque relative to the essence of God.[25] Therefore, in addition to the second-order essence of God there are first-order essences of God. A first-order essence of God is the essence of God insofar as God is conceived or described in strictly one way: for example, God described as the thinking substance. Della Rocca says that 1d4 explicates the opacity of attribute contexts relative to the essence of God. So according to Della Rocca, 1d4 is the statement of the essence of God insofar as God is understood or described in a particular way (i.e. insofar as God is conceived or described as the infinite extended substance or the infinite thinking substance, etc.).[26] Therefore, according to Della Rocca, 1d4 is the statement of first-order essences of God, while 1d6 is the statement of the second-order essence of God.[27]

We know that, for Spinoza, the idea of a thing proceeds from the adequate idea of the essence of the thing. On Della Rocca's account, when the essence of God is conceived via an attribute, the essence of God is conceived in a particular way; that is, the essence of God is conceived insofar as God is conceived as the infinite thinking substance or the infinite extended substance, etc. The de re idea of a thing, that is, the idea of a thing itself, follows from the adequate idea of the essence of the thing. In 2d2 Spinoza says that when that which pertains to the essence of a thing is conceived, the thing is conceived. If each particular attribute satisfies the stipulation of 2d2 relative to the essence of God, then when a particular attribute is conceived, God is conceived. So on this interpretation, the adequate idea of any particular attribute results in the idea of God. If the de re idea of a thing follows only from the adequate idea of the essence of the thing, then one might think that each particular attribute must be the essence of God. That is, since the idea of any particular attribute results in the idea of God, each particular attribute might be viewed as the essence of God. This is exactly what Della Rocca claims; he says that each attribute is the essence of God insofar as God is conceived or described in that particular way. So, on this view, the conception of the attribute of thought or the attribute of extension is the adequate idea of the essence of God for the human intellect.

God

On Della Rocca's interpretation, God has two kinds of essences. The second-order essence of God is constituted by the collection of attributes, and the first-order essences are constituted by each particular attribute. Indeed, on Della Rocca's view *each particular attribute is the essence of God* insofar as God's essence is conceived or described in that particular way. Further, *the collection of attributes is the essence of God* insofar as God is conceived or described in infinite ways.

If God is identical with the essence of God, then on Della Rocca's interpretation God is identical with some particular attribute, or with each particular attribute, or with the collection of attributes. God cannot be identical with some particular attribute, since there is equal reason to claim that God is identical with some other attribute. If God is identical with each particular attribute, then each particular attribute is identical with every other attribute. This is impossible since the attributes are really distinct. Hence, God cannot be identical with each of the particular attributes. God cannot be identical with the collection of attributes since this would render God a divisible entity, i.e. divisible into distinct attributes.

I have suggested that we consider the possibility that a thing is not identical with its essence. If God is not identical with God's essence, then on Della Rocca's interpretation God is not identical with any particular attribute, nor with each particular attribute, nor with the collection of attributes.

On Della Rocca's view, the adequate idea of either of the known attributes is the idea of the essence of God (insofar as God's essence is conceived or described in that way). Hence, on this view the idea of an attribute results in the de re idea of God—since the idea of a thing follows from the idea of the essence of the thing. What is the de re idea of God? Is it just identical with the adequate idea of an attribute of God? Or is the de re idea of God distinct from the idea of an attribute of God? In other words, is God the attributes or something else? The answers to these questions can be found by revisiting the three problems. In doing so we will find that God is something other than the attributes.

Solutions to the three problems

Problem one: the relation of God to the attributes

What is the relationship between God and the attributes? It seems that this relationship cannot be one of identity. We know that God cannot be identical with the totality of indiscrete attributes, since the attributes are really distinct. Furthermore, God cannot be identical with the collection of attributes, since the collection of attributes is divisible into distinct attributes; and God is an indivisible entity. Also, God cannot be identical with each of the particular attributes, since the attributes would then be identical with one another. Therefore, I suggest that God, rather than being identical with the attributes, must be the entity that *has* infinite attributes. Della Rocca says that God can be described as "the substance of infinitely many attributes", and that the essence of God under this description is "being the substance of infinite attributes".[28] These two are not identical. Hence, it seems that Della Rocca would agree with the view that rather than being identical with the attributes, God *has* attributes. So, the relation of God to the attributes is one of possessing or "having" attributes.

Problem two: the essence of God

I have shown that for Spinoza, God cannot be identical with God's essence.[29] The essence of a thing cannot just be the thing, otherwise there would be absolutely no distinction between the two.[30] Hence, there would be no reason to differentiate between them or to employ the term "essence" when it would simply mean "the thing itself".[31] What, then, is the essence of God? Are the attributes the essence of God? 2d2 says that that which pertains to the essence of a thing must be conceived in order to conceive the thing. So, there is something that is necessary and sufficient for the conception of God, such that God is conceived whenever *and only when* it is conceived. This means that the particular attributes are ruled out by 2d2. That is, if each particular attribute is what pertains to the essence of God, then more than one attribute satisfies the stipulations of 2d2 relative to God. This is impossible, since 2d2 says that that which pertains to the essence of a thing is *necessary* for the conception of a thing (i.e. that which pertains to the essence of a thing is that without which the thing can neither be nor be conceived). Therefore, if the attributes pertain to the essence of God, then it would be necessary to conceive all the attributes (or both if there are only two) since they would *all* be necessary for the conception of God. Hence, it is only the collection of attributes that could be considered as a possibility for fulfilling the stipulation of 2d2. We know, however, that the human intellect can have an adequate idea of the essence of God through only one attribute. So, conceiving the collection (even if there are only two) is not necessary for conceiving God.

It seems that something else besides the particular attributes or the collection of attributes must be that which pertains to the essence of God. That which pertains to the essence of a thing is *always* conceived when the thing is conceived, and when the thing is conceived that which pertains to the essence of the thing is *always* conceived. It seems, then, that that which pertains to the essence of a thing must just be the essence of the thing. So, what pertains to the essence of God is just the essence of God. This just means that when the essence of God is given, God is given, and vice versa; and when the essence of God is conceived, God is conceived, and vice versa. Hence, when we conceive the essence of God we conceive God (i.e. the conception of the essence of God is necessary and sufficient for the conception of God). What is the essence of God; what is it that we conceive when we conceive God? In order to answer this question we must consider what it is to be the essence of a thing. Further, we must understand the relation between the essence of God and the attributes.

What is a thing's essence? I have shown that a thing's power is its essence.[32] Indeed, in 1p34 Spinoza says that God's power is God's essence.[33] Certain things necessarily follow from the essence of a thing, and we know that absolutely everything follows from the essence of God.[34] Therefore God's essence is *absolutely infinite and eternal power*. So, absolutely infinite and eternal power satisfies the stipulations of 2d2; absolutely infinite and eternal power is that which pertains to the essence of God. Hence the conception of absolutely infinite and eternal power is necessary and sufficient for the conception of God. How is the essence of God conceived by the human intellect? This leads us to the third problem.

Problem three: the true conception of God

What is the true conception of God, and what role do the attributes play in the conception of God? We know that the conception of God requires the conception of the essence of God. God's power is God's essence. Hence, the human intellect must conceive absolutely infinite and eternal power in order to conceive God. In 1d4 Spinoza says that the attributes are what the intellect perceives as constituting the essence of substance. So when an attribute is conceived, the essence of God (absolutely infinite and eternal power) is conceived. There are at least two attributes. It is reasonable, then, to ask how the same essence (absolutely infinite and eternal power) is conceived through different attributes. In 1p16d Spinoza says that each attribute "expresses an essence infinite in its own kind". According to this demonstration, each attribute is the expression of the essence of God in a particular *kind*; an attribute is a different *way* in which absolutely infinite and eternal power is expressed. So, the essence of God is expressed as absolutely infinite thought, absolutely infinite extension, etc. Della Rocca has captured this aspect of the attributes. He says that each attribute is the essence of God *insofar* as God is conceived or described in that particular way. Indeed, I suggest that the essence of God can be conceived and, hence, described in different ways precisely because the essence of God is *expressed* in particular ways or kinds; it is those very expressions of absolutely infinite and eternal power that are conceived, and hence, described.

Although each attribute is the expression of the essence of God in a particular kind, only one attribute (one way the essence of God is expressed) need be conceived in order to conceive the essence of God; this is because the attributes are parallel in nature. That is, because each attribute expresses the very same essence, everything that is expressed (and therefore conceived) under one attribute is necessarily expressed (and therefore conceived) under any other attribute.[35] Each attribute is simply a different way in which God's essence or power is expressed. The attribute of thought is absolutely infinite and eternal power expressed in a thinking kind, and the attribute of extension is absolutely infinite and eternal power expressed in an extended kind. It is because each attribute expresses absolutely infinite and eternal power (the essence of God) in a particular way or kind that absolutely infinite and eternal power (the essence of God) can be conceived through each attribute. Further, it is because absolutely infinite and eternal power (the essence of God) is conceived in a particular way or kind that absolutely infinite and eternal power (the essence of God) can be described in a particular way or kind. It is that conception (in that way or kind) that is described.

Absolutely infinite and eternal power satisfies the stipulations of 2d2 relative to God. The essence of God is an infinite essence; hence it is expressed in infinite kinds or ways. The essence of God can be conceived through any of the kinds or ways in which it is expressed. Consequently, God can be conceived by the human intellect as the infinite thinking thing or the infinite extended thing. I suggest, therefore, that the collection of attributes is absolutely infinite and eternal power in all kinds, and that each particular attribute is absolutely infinite and eternal power in that particular kind.

We can see a parallel between the essence of modes and the essence of God. Consider a particular mode, for example, human being H. We would not want to say that the endeavor of human mind M to persist in its own being is the essence of H; nor would we want to say that the endeavor of human body B to persist in its own being is the essence of H. Rather, the conatus or power of the mode itself—human being H—is the essence of H. This is the power or essence of the entire entity. This conatus or power of the entire entity, human being H, is, in turn, *expressed* in two kinds or ways: as a mind (or thinking thing), and as a body (or an extended thing). So, the endeavor of human mind M to persist in its own being is the essence or power of H expressed as thought; and the endeavor of human body B to persist in its own being is the essence or power of H expressed as extension. Likewise, we would not want to say that the attribute of thought is the essence of God; nor would we want to say that the attribute of extension is the essence of God. Rather, the power of the unique substance itself is the essence of God. This absolutely infinite and eternal power is, in turn, expressed in infinite kinds: the power or essence of God is expressed as infinite thought (or the infinite intellect), and the power or essence of God is expressed as infinite extension (or the infinite physical universe).[36]

What pertains to the essence of God is absolutely infinite and eternal power. God cannot be conceived without conceiving absolutely infinite and eternal power. Because God's essence or power is *absolutely* infinite, there are infinite kinds or ways in which God's essence is expressed.[37] So, God's essence is expressed as infinite thought, infinite extension, infinite X, infinite Y, etc. Further, God's essence can be conceived through any of the ways in which it is expressed. (It follows that because human beings are expressed under the attributes of thought and extension, God's essence or power can be conceived by the human intellect as absolutely infinite thought or absolutely infinite extension.) When God's essence is conceived, God is conceived. The conception of either of the known attributes by the human intellect is the conception of the essence of God, since the power that is expressed through one attribute is the same power that is expressed through another attribute; it is the same power expressed in two different ways or kinds. God, then, is the entity that has absolutely infinite and eternal power; and God's essence is absolutely infinite and eternal power. Since God's essence is infinite, there are infinite kinds or ways in which absolutely infinite and eternal power is expressed, and hence there are infinite kinds or ways in which absolutely infinite and eternal power is conceived or described. The attributes, then, are the ways God's power is expressed. So, God is conceived by the human intellect via the attributes as the thing that has infinite and eternal power.

The adequate idea of God is the result of the conception of the essence of God via a particular way that essence is expressed. God's essence or power is expressed as absolutely infinite and eternal thinking, absolutely infinite and eternal extension, etc. Letter 36 seems to support this view:

> *And since God's nature does not consist in one definite kind of being*, but in being which is absolutely indeterminate, *his nature also demands*

all that which perfectly expresses being, otherwise his nature would be determinate and deficient. This being so, it follows that there can be only one Being, God, which exists by its own force. For if, let us say, we suppose that Extension involves existence, it must needs be eternal and indeterminate, and express absolutely no imperfection, but only perfection. And so Extension will pertain to God, or will be *something that expresses God's nature in some way*, for God is a Being which is indeterminate in essence and omnipotent absolutely, and not merely in a particular respect.[38]

Spinoza says that God's nature (essence) is absolutely indeterminate, and therefore God's nature (essence) requires everything that perfectly expresses being. Spinoza concludes that the attribute of extension *expresses the essence* of God. I suggest, therefore, that God's essence is absolutely infinite and eternal power, which is indeterminate, and this indeterminate power is expressed in infinite kinds or ways (i.e. as infinite thought, infinite extension, etc.).

God and the attributes

I have suggested that in Spinoza's metaphysics, when the essence of God (E) is "expressed" by an attribute (A) there is a relation between them such that: (1) A is not identical with E, and (2) A is not caused by E, but (3) A is such that E can be conceived through A. I have claimed that this "expression relation" is true of the attributes and God's essence. If the attributes express the essence of God, then (1) the attributes are not identical with the essence of God, and (2) the attributes are not caused by the essence of God, but (3) the essence of God can be conceived through the attributes.

God is the being or thing that has absolutely infinite and eternal power; and God's essence *is* absolutely infinite and eternal power. Since God's essence is infinite, there are infinite ways in which absolutely infinite and eternal power is expressed, and hence conceived or described. That is, the essence or power of God can be conceived by the infinite intellect via any of the ways it is expressed, and by the human intellect via two of the ways it is expressed, viz.

thought and extension. The attributes, then, are the ways God's power is expressed.

The definition of God

For Spinoza, there is a necessary relation between a thing's essence and the definition of a thing. Now we have the solutions to the three problems associated with God and the attributes in Spinoza's metaphysics. We can go on, then, to inquire whether this interpretation of God, God's essence, and the attributes correlates with Spinoza's definition of God.

For Spinoza, the essence of a thing is given by the definition of the thing; that is, the definition of a thing simply is the statement of the essence of the thing: "For the definition of any thing affirms, and does not deny, the thing's essence, *or* it posits the thing's essence, and does not take it away."[39] Indeed, "the true definition of each thing neither involves nor expresses anything except the nature of the thing defined."[40] So, Spinoza's definition of God should be the statement of the essence of God. 1d6 is Spinoza's definition of God:

> By God I understand a being absolutely infinite, i.e., a substance consisting of an infinity of attributes, of which each one expresses an eternal and infinite essence.

The explication of 1d6 makes it clear that God is not an entity infinite only in its own kind; rather, God is an *absolutely* infinite being.[41] Therefore, "whatever expresses essence and involves no negation pertains to [God's] essence".

When the definition of God is addressed in the literature on Spinoza's metaphysics it is mainly from the view that the definition of a thing is the statement of the thing's essence and that the essence of a thing involves the thing's cause. This is a commonly held view, since Spinoza tells us in 1a4 that any effect is known through its cause, and Spinoza holds the view that any particular thing *is* the effect of some cause.[42] Hence, knowledge of a thing entails knowledge of the thing's cause. Also, according to 2d2 a thing is conceived via its essence. So, the conception of a thing involves both the thing's cause and the thing's essence. Della Rocca, among many others, holds this view. For example, he says that "x's essence includes x's cause" is "a shorthand way of making the point that x's essence consists in being that cause's effect", and that "we can say that the essence of x consists in being the effect of a certain cause".[43] Since God is self-caused, the definition of God involves no external cause. Curley agrees when he says that the definition of God must exclude every cause except for God.[44] These discussions of definition, essence, and cause have laid a robust foundation for further inquiry into Spinoza's definition of God. But there is a neglected question about 1d6: whether it is an adequate definition of Spinoza's God. This is an important question that has not been explored in the literature. In 2p10s2 Spinoza says: "The essence is what the thing can neither be nor be conceived without, and vice versa, what can neither be nor be conceived without the thing." So, according to Spinoza's metaphysics, the definition of a thing should capture the essence of the thing, and to have an adequate idea of a thing is to conceive it through its essence.[45] Hence, there is an important relation between an adequate definition of God and an adequate idea of God—an adequate idea of God arises from an idea of what is stated in an adequate definition of God (i.e. from the idea of the essence of God).

If 1d6 is not an adequate definition of God, then there is a serious problem in Spinoza's metaphysics. The problem is that we cannot know for sure what we must conceive in order to have an adequate idea of God, since we must conceive what is stated in an adequate definition of God, and in this case we would have an inadequate statement of the essence of God. If we do not know what must be conceived in order to conceive God, then we can never know if one has an adequate idea of God. If 1d6 is not an adequate definition of God, then a very important tenet of Spinoza's metaphysical doctrine is discredited. Spinoza claims that the human mind *does* have an adequate idea of the essence of God. How can we know what this idea is, if it is not the idea of what is stated in the definition of God? If, on the other hand, 1d6 *is* an adequate definition of God, then the question we must ask is: what is it to conceive "a being absolutely infinite", or "a substance consisting of an infinity of attributes, of which each one expresses an eternal and infinite essence"? As we know, many commentators hold the view that the attributes are the essence of God. On this view, of course, the conception of God involves the conception of at least one attribute. 1d6 says that God has an infinity of attributes (of which we know two, viz. thought and extension). The idea that we must conceive *an* attribute in order to conceive God doesn't seem to correlate well with the idea that an adequate conception of God involves the conception of what is stated in the definition of God (since the definition refers to an *infinity* of attributes). 1d6 seems to imply that the idea of God requires the idea of an infinite number of attributes. Although the infinite intellect is capable of having this idea, the human mind is not. If it can be shown that conceiving God involves conceiving any *particular* attribute, then we need to know how conceiving *an* attribute is the conception of "a being absolutely infinite", or "a substance consisting of an infinity of attributes".

I will approach the topic of the definition of God and its relation to the idea of God by posing three questions about 1d6. First, we can ask whether 1d6 correlates with 1p34, which says that God's *power* is God's essence. If 1d6 does comport with 1p34, then it seems that 1d6 should say something about God's *power*, since 1d6 is the statement of the essence of God and Spinoza says that *power* is God's essence. Second, the human intellect has an adequate idea of God's essence through either the attribute of thought or the attribute of extension, and that is the only way we can have an adequate idea of the essence of God (since we can conceive only these two attributes).[46] 1d6, however, mentions attributes only generically and does not mention any particular attribute. So, another question we can ask is whether the definition of God should concern the attribute of thought or the attribute of extension or (possibly) both. This, in turn, leads us to the third question. How can there be an adequate idea of God that involves only one attribute if the definition of God, which captures God's essence, mentions more than one attribute and an idea of a thing can be adequate only if it involves the conception of the thing's essence?

We have inquired into key doctrines in Spinoza's metaphysics. In doing so we have found that the conception of the essence of a thing is what is necessary and sufficient for the conception of the thing. Also, I have shown that according to Spinoza's claims in 1p34 and 3p7 a thing's power is identical with its essence. Further, we know that for Spinoza an "adequate idea" is internal to the mind that has it. Finally, I have shown that the relation between the attributes and the essence of God is a relation of *expression*. Let us now consider how understanding these key doctrines helps in answering the three questions about Spinoza's definition of God.

Does 1d6 correlate with 1p34 (which says that God's *power* is God's essence), and if so, should 1d6 say something about God's *power*? I have shown that for Spinoza a thing's power is identical with its essence. This means that the definition of a thing should state what its power is. For example, if we want to know the essence of human being H, then we must discover the definition that accurately states the power of H. The definition of H will describe a particular, unique, finite power. Spinoza's definition of God, on the other hand, should capture the notion of God's power (i.e. the power of the absolutely infinite and eternal substance). The power of absolutely infinite and eternal substance is absolutely infinite and eternal power, and absolutely infinite and eternal power is necessarily expressed in infinite ways. 1d6 *does* correlate with 1p34, since only one being necessarily expresses its essence in infinite ways; that is the being whose essence *is* absolutely infinite power— not a being whose power is limited in any way. The claim in 1p34 that power is God's essence confirms Spinoza's statement of the essence of God, since only a being whose essence is infinite power could be the being whose essence is expressed infinitely. Hence, 1d6 does say something about God's power; it tells us that God's essence is absolutely infinite and eternal power and that this power necessarily entails its expression.[47]

Since the only way the human intellect has an adequate idea of God's essence is through either the attribute of thought or the attribute of extension, should the definition of God concern the attribute of thought or the attribute of extension or (possibly) both? Spinoza's key doctrines will help us answer this question. Recall that for Spinoza, in order to conceive a thing we must conceive its essence, and a thing's essence is identical with its power. Further, the relation between the attributes and the essence of God is a relation of *expression*—the attributes express God's power. In addition, the idea of the attributes of thought and extension are internal to the human mind, and thus they are adequate ideas in the human mind. So, the human mind has an adequate idea of God via the adequate idea of God's essence (power) through either the attribute of thought or the attribute of extension. How, exactly, does this work?

Since a thing's essence is identical with its power, when we conceive a thing's essence we conceive its power. God's essence is absolutely infinite and eternal power. Hence, in order to conceive God we must conceive absolutely infinite and eternal power. We conceive a thing's power through the expression of that power. We conceive God's power through the expressions of that power (i.e. through the attributes). Absolutely infinite and eternal power can be conceived via any particular attribute, since each of the attributes expresses the very same essence (i.e. the essence or power of God). Therefore, no particular attribute (or attributes) need be conceived in order to conceive God, since God's power may be conceived via any of the ways it is expressed (the attributes of thought and extension being two of those ways). Specific attributes need not be mentioned in the definition of God since absolutely infinite and eternal power is the essence of God and *that* is what we must conceive in order to have an adequate idea of God. That is, we must conceive neither any particular attribute nor all of the attributes, but we must conceive *the essence of God.*

How can there be an adequate idea of God that involves only one attribute if the definition of God, which captures God's essence, mentions more than one attribute? The adequate idea of God proceeds from the idea of the essence of God. The essence of God may be conceived via any attribute, since the attributes are that which the intellect perceives as constituting the essence of God. The attributes are mentioned generically because it is not the conception of absolutely infinite and eternal power in any specific way or kind (i.e. as thought or as extension) that is necessary for having an idea of God. Rather, it is just the conception of *the essence of God* that is necessary and sufficient for having an idea of God. This conception is possible through any attribute, because absolutely infinite and eternal power can be conceived through any of the kinds or ways in which that power is expressed, since it is the very same power that is expressed via each attribute. Indeed, Spinoza tells us in 2p1s that we can conceive God via any particular attribute.[48]

In 1d6 Spinoza says that God is "a being absolutely infinite, i.e., a substance consisting of an infinity of attributes, of which each one expresses an eternal and infinite essence". What is it to conceive "a being absolutely infinite", or "a substance consisting of an infinity of attributes, of which each one expresses an eternal and infinite essence"? We know that the idea of a thing proceeds from the idea of its essence. Therefore, to conceive "a being absolutely infinite", or "a substance consisting of an infinity of attributes, of which each one expresses an eternal and infinite essence", is to conceive that being through its essence. God is the being of which 1d6 is the definition—the statement of the essence of God. Therefore, we must conceive the being, God, through God's essence. God's essence is absolutely infinite and eternal power.

2d2 is the definition of the essence of a thing and the essence of God is absolutely infinite and eternal power; hence, absolutely infinite and eternal power satisfies the stipulation of 2d2 relative to the essence of God. So, when absolutely infinite and eternal power is given, God is given; and when absolutely infinite and eternal power is taken away, God is taken away. Also, when God is given, absolutely infinite and eternal power is given; and when God is taken away, absolutely infinite and eternal power is taken away. The same applies to the conception of God. So, when absolutely infinite and eternal power is conceived, God is conceived; and when absolutely infinite and eternal power is not conceived, God is not conceived. Also, when God is conceived, absolutely infinite and eternal power is conceived; and when God is not conceived, absolutely infinite and eternal power is not conceived. Therefore, the conception of absolutely infinite and eternal power is necessary and sufficient for the conception of God. So we must conceive God's power in order to conceive God. How does the human mind have this idea? The human mind has the idea of God by conceiving God's essence via the expression of that essence (i.e. via the attributes).

I have argued against a prevailing view that the essence of God is somehow identical with the attributes, and I have concluded that *absolutely infinite and eternal power* is God's essence. Indeed, I have claimed that while the attributes do not satisfy the stipulations of 2d2 relative to God, absolutely infinite and eternal power does satisfy those stipulations. I have shown that the definition of "God" (1d6) and the definition of "essence" (2d2) are compatible with Spinoza's propositional claim about the essence of God (1p34). Finally, I have concluded that 1d6 is an adequate definition of God.

The de re idea of God

The human intellect comprehends the essence of God through the expressions of God's power. As modes under the attributes of thought and extension, human beings have access to knowledge of the essence of God through those expressions of God's essence. What is necessary for the de re conception of a thing is the conception of the essence of the thing. Conceiving an attribute is conceiving the essence of God expressed in that particular way or kind. What is conceived through one attribute is conceived through any other attribute. That is, since each attribute expresses the very same power or essence, the conception of any particular attribute is adequate for the conception of the essence of God. Hence, the conception of the essence of God through its expression via a given particular attribute results in the de re idea of God.

On the view that God is identical with the collection of attributes the problem of the divisibility of God arises. My interpretation of God, the essence of God, and the attributes avoids the problem of the divisibility of God. On my view God is the indivisible entity that has attributes, the essence of God is absolutely infinite and eternal power which is expressed in infinite kinds or ways, and the attributes are the kinds or ways in which the essence of God is expressed. This interpretation also avoids the problem incurred by the interpretation of God as the totality of attributes; namely, that the attributes are indistinct. On my view the attributes are distinct kinds or ways in which the essence of God is expressed.

Notes

Introduction

1. A particular concern will be whether the commentators are successful in addressing the three problems in their interpretations without straying too far from the text.
2. 2d2: "I say that to the essence of any thing belongs that which, being given, the thing is [NS: also] necessarily posited and which, being taken away, the thing is necessarily [NS: also] taken away; or that without which the thing can neither be nor be conceived, and which can neither be nor be conceived without the thing." Unless otherwise noted, all quoted passages from the *Ethics* and Spinoza's correspondence are from Edwin Curley (ed. and trans.), *The Collected Works of Spinoza*, vol. 1 (Princeton, NJ: Princeton University Press, 1985).
3. The problem of the divisibility of God will be discussed in detail in Chapter 3.
4. Although I agree with Parchment's initial approach to the question of the relation of God to the attributes, I show in my critique of Parchment that his interpretation collapses into a view that is refutable, given Spinoza's claims about the conception of God and the distinction between the attributes.
5. 1d6: "By God I understand a being absolutely infinite, i.e., a substance consisting of an infinity of attributes, of which each one expresses an eternal and infinite essence.

    Exp: I say absolutely infinite, not infinite in its own kind; for if something is only infinite in its own kind, we can deny infinite attributes of it [NS: (i.e., we can conceive infinite attributes which do not pertain to its nature)]; but if something is absolutely infinite, whatever expresses essence and involves no negation pertains to its essence."

    1p34: "God's power is his essence itself."

Chapter 1: Three Problems

1. My interpretation of God and the attributes will easily accommodate claims like these.
2. 1d6: "By God I understand a being absolutely infinite, i.e., a substance consisting of an infinity of attributes, of which each one expresses an eternal and infinite essence.

Exp: I say absolutely infinite, not infinite in its own kind; for if something is only infinite in its own kind, we can deny infinite attributes of it [NS: (i.e., we can conceive infinite attributes which do not pertain to its nature)]; but if something is absolutely infinite, whatever expresses essence and involves no negation pertains to its essence."

3. See 2p7s, and Letter 64 in *Baruch Spinoza: The Letters* trans. Samuel Shirley (Indianapolis: Hackett Publishing Company, 1995), pp. 298–300.
4. This is a view that might be held by those who claim that God is identical with the attributes.
5. Adequate and true ideas will be discussed in Chapter 6.
6. Indeed, this conclusion follows even if God is not identical with the attributes in any form or combination.
7. 1p14: "Except God, no substance can be or be conceived."

Chapter 2: The "God Is the Thing that Has Attributes and Modes as Properties" Interpretation

1. Jonathan Bennett, *A Study of Spinoza's Ethics* (Indianapolis: Hackett Publishing Company, 1984), pp. 59–61.
2. Ibid., p. 61.
3. Ibid., pp. 75–77.
4. Ibid., p. 62.
5. Ibid., p. 63.
6. Ibid., pp. 62–63.
7. Ibid., p. 64. Bennett argues that an attribute cannot be substance since there are two attributes and only one substance.
8. Ibid., p. 147.
9. 2p7s: "So also a mode of extension and the idea of that mode are one and the same thing, but expressed in two ways."
10. Substance and attribute are not identical entities for Bennett. Indeed, the attributes cannot be identical with God since the attributes are less basic than the trans-attribute differentiae, whereas God is not.
11. Bennett, *A Study of Spinoza's Ethics*, pp. 61, 147.
12. Indeed, on Bennett's interpretation "what the intellect perceives of a substance *as if* constituting its essence" is just fine as a translation too: ibid., p. 146.
13. Ibid.
14. Ibid., p. 61.
15. Ibid., p. 63.
16. Ibid., pp. 61, 147.
17. Ibid., p. 146.
18. Ibid. Bennett argues that even the infinite intellect cannot have an idea of the essence of God, i.e. the modes in abstraction from the attributes.

19. Michael Della Rocca, *Representation and the Mind–Body Problem in Spinoza* (New York: Oxford University Press, 1996), p. 121.
20. Ibid., p. 163.

Chapter 3: The "God Is the Collection of Attributes" Interpretation

1. 1p4d: "Therefore, there is nothing outside the intellect through which a number of things can be distinguished from one another except substances, *or* what is the same (by D4), their attributes, and their affections, q.e.d."
2. Edwin Curley, *Spinoza's Metaphysics* (Cambridge, Mass.: Harvard University Press, 1969), pp. 16–17.
3. Ibid., pp. 16, 144.
4. Ibid., pp. 16–17.
5. Ibid., p. 91.
6. Ibid., p. 19.
7. If God is the collection of *distinct* attributes, then the attributes are parts of God. Hence, on this view, it seems that God is composed of parts. Also, see Bennett's critique of the "God is the collection of attributes" view: Jonathan Bennett, *A Study of Spinoza's Ethics* (Indianapolis: Hackett Publishing Company, 1984), p. 64.
8. Michael J. Loux, *Metaphysics* (London: Routledge, 1998), p. 99.
9. Many commentators would also count the modes among God's qualities, but Curley does not.
10. It seems that if Spinoza had been making this strong claim (i.e. that God is identical with the bundle or collection of distinct attributes) then he would have been more explicit and forward about his stance. Indeed, it would have been philosophically bold for Spinoza to suggest that a thing can be identified simply with its qualities, attributes, or properties.
11. I will use "particular attribute", "distinct attribute", and "discrete attribute" as equivalent terms.
12. Curley, *Spinoza's Metaphysics*, p. 47.
13. Edwin Curley, *Behind the Geometrical Method* (Princeton, NJ: Princeton University Press, 1988), p. 28.
14. Ibid., p. 28.
15. Ibid., p. 43.
16. I will use "the sum of distinct attributes", "the collection of the attributes", and "collection of attributes" as equivalent terms.
17. Remember that under Curley's interpretation, the collection of the attributes is both God and *the* essence of God. Hence, if one can conceive the essence of the collection of the attributes through one attribute, then one can conceive both the essence of God and God (i.e. the collection of attributes) via one attribute.
18. 1p10: "Each attribute of a substance must be conceived through itself."

19. 1p10 and the demonstration state that because an attribute is what the intellect perceives as constituting the essence of a substance (and a substance is conceived only through itself), each attribute must be conceived through itself alone. So it seems impossible that the essence of the collection of distinct attributes can be conceived through one attribute alone; and certainly, if the intellect perceives truly then the attributes *are* distinct from one another.
20. Indeed, Curley holds this view. See *Spinoza's Metaphysics*, p. 150, where Curley says that the intellect referred to in 1d4 is the infinite intellect.
21. Baruch Spinoza, *The Ethics and Selected Letters*, ed. Seymour Feldman, trans. Samuel Shirley (Indianapolis: Hackett Publishing Company, 1982), pp. 93–94.
22. 1a4: "The knowledge of an effect depends on, and involves, the knowledge of its cause."; 1p15: "Whatever is, is in God, and nothing can be or be conceived without God."
23. 2p46d: "The demonstration of the preceding Proposition is Universal, and whether the thing is considered as a part or as a whole, its idea, whether of the whole or a part (by P45), will involve God's eternal and infinite essence."
24. 2p7: "The order and connection of ideas is the same as the order and connection of things."
25. That is, the conception of an infinite thinking being *is* the conception of God, unless it is a false conception.
26. Curley, *Behind the Geometrical Method*, pp. 28–30.
27. Ibid., p. 28: "So our conception of God as supremely perfect forces us to accept as legitimate the conception of a being possessing infinitely many attributes or essences."
28. Ibid., p. 43. Here Curley says that the entire collection of attributes is the essence of God.
29. Both God and *the* essence of God are the collection of attributes, according to Curley.
30. 1p10s: "From these propositions it is evident that although two attributes may be conceived to be really distinct (i.e., one may be conceived without the aid of the other), we still can not infer from that that they constitute two beings, *or* two different substances."
31. Certainly, the view that God is many entities does not seem right, since a thing can be identical only with itself. So, if a thing and its essence are identical entities then there is really only one thing. Hence, if God has many essences then those essences and God itself are all identical entities. So there are not many essences, there is only one essence. And there are not many entities, there is only one entity.
32. This is impossible on Curley's view if there are more than two attributes; further, it is unnecessary to conceive more than one attribute according to 2p1s.
33. One could claim that the adequate idea of *an* essence of God is the adequate

conception of *the* essence of the collection, since there is nothing expressed under one attribute that is not also expressed under every other attribute. So, the essence perceived via any particular attribute is identical with the essence perceived via all of the other attributes. This, however, does not give us an idea of the collection of *distinct* attributes. Further, the question whether the collection of attributes is identical with God is not answered by this reading of *an* essence and *the* essence of God.

34. Jonathan Bennett, *A Study of Spinoza's Ethics* (Indianapolis: Hackett Publishing Company, 1984), p. 64.
35. Alan Donagan, *Spinoza* (Chicago: University of Chicago Press, 1988), pp. 69–70, 83.
36. Ibid., pp. 88–89.
37. Donagan says that if an attribute is identical with the essence of a substance of one attribute, then the attribute is identical with the substance; hence, Donagan assumes that the essence of the substance is identical with the substance. There are, however, those who would hold that the essence of a thing is not identical with the thing.
38. Ibid., p. 89.
39. This would seem to be the case given Donagan's claim that the attribute of a substance of one attribute is identical with the essence of that substance and hence with the substance itself.
40. Alan Donagan, "Essence and the Distinction of Attributes", in *Spinoza: A Collection of Critical Essays*, ed. Marjorie Grene (Notre Dame, Ind.: University of Notre Dame Press, 1973), pp. 180–81.
41. Donagan, *Spinoza*, p. 59. Della Rocca agrees with this reading of 2d2: see Michael Della Rocca, *Representation and the Mind–Body Problem in Spinoza* (New York: Oxford University Press, 1996), p. 186 n. 1. The meaning of 2d2 will be discussed in detail in Chapter 6.
42. I discuss the problem of the divisibility of a substance in greater detail at the end of Chapter 4, where I discuss the benefits and disadvantages of the "God is the collection of attributes" view.
43. This is a view that is held by other Spinoza scholars; see, for example, Della Rocca, pp. 157, 167.
44. Donagan, *Spinoza*, pp. 69–70: "Finally, since the essence of a substance is an individual, attributes as Spinoza conceives them are not properties, but individuals."
45. Donagan, "Essence and the Distinction of Attributes", p. 177.
46. Ibid., pp. 180–81. The complications of this stance will be discussed in my interpretation of the essence of substance in Chapter 6.
47. Donagan, *Spinoza*, pp. 88–89.
48. See Donagan, "Essence and the Distinction of Attributes", p. 177.
49. Donagan, *Spinoza*, p. 88.
50. Ibid., p. 89.

Chapter 4: The "God Is the Totality of Attributes" Interpretation

1. H. F. Hallett, *Benedict De Spinoza: The Elements of His Philosophy* (London: Athlone Press, 1957), pp. 9, 19.
2. Ibid., p. 19.
3. Ibid., p. 28.
4. 3d2: "I say that we act when something happens, in us or outside us, of which we are the adequate cause, i.e. (by D1), when something in us or outside us follows from our nature, which can be clearly and distinctly understood through it alone. On the other hand, I say that we are acted on when something happens in us, or something follows from our nature, of which we are only a partial cause."
5. "By 'action' is signified the distinction in unity of 'potency' and its 'actuality'. For to say that something is 'actual' is to imply that it is the determinate actuality of some potency-in-act. Agency involves both a power of act*ing* and the expression of that power in something enact*ed*, a doing and a deed, and in action *par excellence* that which is enacted is the exhaustive expression of the potency, without inhibition or frustration, by which agency may otherwise be reduced to durational effort more or less effective. Action is thus originally and essentially eternal, and becomes durational only by limitation and modification. Mere uniform temporal sequence can be styled 'causality' only by way of paradox—*lucas a non lucendo*": Hallett, *Benedict De Spinoza*, p. 9.
6. Ibid., p. 28.
7. Ibid., p. 16.
8. "The *conceived* (and truly conceived) distinctions of the infinite Attributes of Substance is thus with respect to the actualization of one of them, viz. Thought. Substance as such suffers no such distinction, nevertheless these distinctions are valid since from its very nature as potency-in-act Substance exists only as self-actualizing—as producing infinite things 'in infinite ways'. It may be objected that it is paradoxical to say that Substance is both absolutely indeterminate and also 'consists of infinite Attributes'—and indeed it would be so if the nature of Substance provided no 'logical room' for this disparity, if, for example, Substance were a 'thing' and not an *agent*. The apparent contradiction is 'dialectical' or self-resolved in the conception of creative agency": ibid., p. 18.
9. "The Attribute *is* the Substance under the determining scrutiny of intellect": ibid., p. 16. For more on Hallett's view on the attributes, see ibid., pp. 16–23.
10. Ibid., p. 18. This is a confusing tenet that I will consider in greater detail when I discuss Steven Parchment's view on God and the attributes later in this chapter.
11. Ibid., p. 20.
12. Ibid.
13. Ibid.

14. Ibid., pp. 18, 22.
15. Ibid., p. 17.
16. Ibid., p. 19. Hallett holds the view that there is no multiplicity of essences of God.
17. Ibid., p. 20.
18. I will use the terms "indiscerptible", "indistinct", and "indiscrete" interchangeably.
19. Indeed, according to Hallett, the attributes do not form any infinite collection.
20. See 1p10s.
21. 1p10: "Each attribute of a substance must be conceived through itself.
    Dem.: For an attribute is what the intellect perceives concerning a substance, as constituting its essence (by D4); so (by D3) it must be conceived through itself, q.e.d."
22. 2p32: "All ideas, insofar as they are related to God, are true."
23. 2p34: "Every idea that in us is absolute, or adequate and perfect, is true."
24. Steven Parchment, "The God/Attribute Distinction in Spinoza's Metaphysics: A Defense of Causal Objectivism", *History of Philosophy Quarterly* 13 (1996), pp. 55–72.
25. Parchment suggests that on the standard objectivist interpretation, the reference to the intellect in 1d4 is unnecessary since, on this reading, an attribute will constitute the essence of God regardless of the perception of the attributes by the intellect. It seems, however, that the intellect is included in 1d4 since the intellect cannot perceive God in abstraction from the attributes. Rather, the intellect perceives God only through the differentiated attributes. Although the attributes are not ontologically dependent on the intellect, the attributes *are* what the intellect perceives of God. Hence, Spinoza includes the intellect in his definition of attribute.
26. Ibid., p. 66.
27. Ibid., p. 55, and see p. 55 n. 4.
28. Ibid., p. 70 n. 28.
29. Ibid., p. 63.
30. Ibid., p. 66.
31. Ibid., p. 63. The "totality of the attributes" is a unity wherein the particular attributes are undiscoverable.
32. Ibid., p. 55. Here Parchment says: "Objectivists commonly interpret the divine essence as a collection of distinct attributes. But the idea of a collection of attributes is conceptually derivative and divisible, whereas God is in essence conceptually prior (ID3) and indivisible (IP13)." It appears, at this point, as though Parchment might be conflating God and the divine essence. Parchment cites 1d3, which is the definition of a substance, i.e. the statement of the essence of a substance. However, he then cites 1p13. 1p13 discusses the indivisibility of a substance, not the indivisibility of the essence of a substance. Also, on p. 55 n. 4 Parchment says: "There is no necessity that an objectivist

understand the divine essence as a collection of attributes. The interpretation I wish to establish . . . does not view God as an attributive aggregate." Here again, Parchment seems to be discussing both God and the divine essence in terms of the question of aggregation. Parchment has not shown, however, that whatever can be said of God necessarily can be said of the divine essence. This apparent conflation will be discussed further in my critique of Parchment's interpretation.

33. Ibid., pp. 63–64.
34. Ibid., p. 64.
35. Ibid., pp. 61–62.
36. Ibid., p. 61.
37. Ibid., pp. 56, 62, 64. It seems odd to claim that the attributes are not self-caused. Spinoza explains in 1p10s that the attributes cannot be produced by one another and that "each expresses the reality, *or* being of substance". In the demonstration of 1p10 Spinoza explains that, since each attribute does express the being of substance and a substance must be conceived through itself, each attribute must be conceived through itself. It follows that, since a substance is caused by itself, each attribute must be caused by itself. If some attribute were not caused by itself, then some attribute would not express the being of substance. Indeed, Spinoza claims that the attributes are really distinct from one another, and Parchment has shown that a real distinction entails both conceptual and ontological independence.
38. See René Descartes, *The Philosophical Writings of Descartes*, trans. John Cottingham, Robert Stoothoff, and Dugald Murdoch, vol. 1 (New York: Cambridge University Press, 1985), pp. 213–15, and Parchment, "The God/Attribute Distinction in Spinoza's Metaphysics", pp. 56–57.
39. Spinoza does not endorse Descartes' theory in its entirety, since Descartes thinks that conceivability apart from each other and any other thing entails a real distinction between two different substances, whereas Spinoza allows that the attributes are conceivable apart from each other but are not different substances. Parchment himself admits that Spinoza cannot endorse the whole theory as it stands.
40. Ibid., p. 57.
41. Ibid., p. 59.
42. Ibid., pp. 57–59.
43. Ibid., p. 62.
44. This just means that a distinction of reason entails identity, not that all identities are examples of distinctions of reason.
45. Ibid., p. 62.
46. Ibid.
47. Ibid., p. 63.
48. Ibid.
49. Ibid., p. 62.

50. Ibid., p. 63.
51. Ibid., p. 62.
52. See 2p45–47.
53. "A particular attribute cannot pertain to or constitute the essence of God": Parchment, "The God/Attribute Distinction in Spinoza's Metaphysics", p. 61.
54. See Descartes, *The Philosophical Writings of Descartes*, vol. 1, pp. 214–15.
55. See the discussion earlier in the chapter of "Hallett and the three problems".
56. This problem will be discussed in greater detail in "The totality as homogenized" section later in the chapter.
57. Parchment, "The God/Attribute Distinction in Spinoza's Metaphysics", p. 61.
58. Ibid., pp. 63–64.
59. "X pertains to the essence of Y if and only if X can neither be nor be conceived without Y and Y can neither be nor be conceived without X. In other words, there is a mutual conceptual and ontological dependence": ibid., p. 61.
60. "Spinoza does claim that the totality of attributes pertains to substance (1P19D) and constitutes the divine essence (1P20D)": ibid.
61. Ibid., p. 61 and n. 24.
62. Ibid., p. 62.
63. See the "Critique of interpretive option one" section earlier in the chapter.
64. On Parchment's interpretation the totality of attributes satisfies the stipulations of 2d2.
65. Parchment, "The God/Attribute Distinction in Spinoza's Metaphysics", p. 65.
66. Ibid., p. 61. Nor, on the second interpretive option, is the totality of attributes the essence of God.
67. Ibid., p. 62.
68. "'Tanquam' should be translated 'as if' because no one attribute really constitutes the essence of substance": ibid., p. 66.
69. For Parchment, the totality of attributes is not made up of distinct attributes. So Parchment may claim that the essence of the totality of attributes is a singular essence whose conception does not involve the conception of particular attributes.
70. See Michael Della Rocca, *Representation and the Mind–Body Problem in Spinoza* (New York: Oxford University Press, 1996), p. 157: "Spinoza does, after all, insist that the attributes are conceived to be really distinct (1p10s). Such a conception is certainly, for Spinoza, one that the infinite intellect has, for in 2p7s Spinoza speaks of the infinite intellect perceiving attributes as constituting the essence of substance. Now, for Spinoza, . . . the conceptions of an infinite intellect must all be true. Thus, in conceiving the attributes as distinct, the infinite intellect is conceiving them truly."
71. Indeed, on the first interpretive option God, too, is an entity composed of the homogenized attributes.

72. I discussed this claim in Chapter 2. In 2p1s Spinoza tells us that we can conceive God through one attribute: "So since we can conceive an infinite: Being by attending to thought alone, Thought (by 1d4 and 1d6) is necessarily one of God's infinite attributes." Spinoza has already proved (in 1p14) that there exists only one substance and that substance is God. Hence, the infinite being that is conceived through thought alone must be the unique infinite being, i.e. God. Moreover, Spinoza concludes in 2p1s that thought is an attribute of God, i.e. the unique infinite being. So, the human intellect can have an adequate idea of God through the attribute of thought alone. Since the attributes are parallel in nature, it follows that the human intellect can have an adequate idea of God through the attribute of extension alone. That is, by 2p7, everything that is expressed under any particular attribute is also expressed under every other attribute. Hence, if the human intellect can have an adequate idea of God via the attribute of thought, then the human intellect can have an adequate idea of God via any other attribute. So (by 2p1s and 2p47) the human intellect has an adequate idea of the essence of God through either the attribute of thought or the attribute of extension.

Chapter 5: Benefits and Disadvantages of the Three Interpretations

1. These problems will be addressed later in the chapter, when I discuss the interpretations of Curley, Donagan, Hallett, and Parchment.
2. See 1p4d and Letter 9.
3. The first part of 1p12d reads: "For the parts into which a substance so conceived would be divided either will retain the nature of the substance or will not. If the first [NS: viz. they retain the nature of the substance], then (by P8) each part will have to be infinite, and (by P7) its own cause, and (by P5) each part will have to consist of a different attribute. And so many substances will be able to be formed from one, which is absurd (by P6). Furthermore, the parts (by P2) would have nothing in common with their whole, and the whole (by D4 and P10) could both be and be conceived without its parts, which is absurd, as no one will be able to doubt."
4. See Chapter 4 n. 37 for a discussion of the self-causation of attributes.
5. Edwin Curley, *Behind the Geometrical Method* (Princeton, NJ: Princeton University Press, 1988), p. 28.
6. H. F. Hallett, *Benedict De Spinoza: The Elements of His Philosophy* (London: Athlone Press, 1957), p. 18.
7. Hallett, *Benedict De Spinoza*, pp. 16, 20.
8. Ibid., p. 20.
9. Steven Parchment, "The God/Attribute Distinction in Spinoza's Metaphysics: A Defense of Causal Objectivism", *History of Philosophy Quarterly* 13 (1996), p. 61. Here Parchment says, "the definition of 'pertaining to the essence of' is articulated in IID2 in terms of a *distinctio rationis*. X pertains to

the essence of Y if and only if X can neither be nor be conceived without Y and Y can neither be nor be conceived without X. In other words, there is a mutual conceptual and ontological dependence."
10. See 2p45–47.
11. This must be the case, that is, because the human intellect cannot have a direct idea of the totality of attributes. This is because, on the totality of attributes view, the attributes are not distinct from one another (and the human intellect cannot perceive the attributes as indistinct from one another), and because the human intellect cannot perceive more than two attributes.
12. This must be the case because the idea of a particular attribute itself cannot give rise to the idea of God (i.e. on Parchment's view particular attributes do not satisfy the stipulations of 2d2).

Chapter 6: Essences and True Ideas in Spinoza

1. See 2p47.
2. "Pertinere" in 2d2 may be interpreted as "belongs" or "pertains".
3. For example, see Steven Parchment, "The God/Attribute Distinction in Spinoza's Metaphysics: A Defense of Causal Objectivism", *History of Philosophy Quarterly* 13 (1996), p. 69 n. 24.
4. For example, see Alan Donagan, *Spinoza* (Chicago: University of Chicago Press, 1988), p. 89.
5. Jonathan Bennett, *A Study of Spinoza's Ethics* (Indianapolis: Hackett Publishing Company, 1984), p. 61.
6. Ibid., p. 65.
7. It may actually be the case that Bennett interprets "constitute" in 1p10s differently than the way he interprets the term relative to the essence of a thing. Bennett says that 1d4 indicates that the intellect falsely perceives the attributes as constituting the essence of God (see ibid., p. 146). That is why Bennett thinks that interpreting "tanquam" as "as if" in 1d4 is a good translation, i.e. the intellect perceives the attributes "as if" they constitute the essence of God. If "constitute" in this definition simply means fixes, defines, or determines, then it is difficult to see what Bennett's concern is regarding 1d4. It seems, rather, that Bennett must be taking "constitute" in 1d4 to mean "identical with"; so the intellect falsely perceives the attributes as identical with the essence of God. Since Bennett does not think that the attributes are identical with God's essence, it is easy to see why he would be seriously concerned with 1d4 only if he takes "constitute" to be synonymous with "identical with" in this definition. It is not clear why there would be a problem with 1d4 on Bennett's view if the definition means that the intellect perceives the attributes as fixing, defining, or determining the essence of God, since on his view the attributes are the closest the intellect can get to an idea of the essence of God. Although Bennett may indeed interpret the term "consti-

tute" differently in 1p10s and 1d4, it is unclear why he thinks this is legitimate. That is, in the first case (1p10s) he interprets the term as *not* meaning "identical with", and in the second case (1d4) it seems that he interprets the term as meaning "identical with". However, these opposite interpretations are grounded in the very same reason, i.e. because he does not think that substance is identical with its attributes.

8. Edwin Curley, *Behind the Geometrical Method* (Princeton, NJ: Princeton University Press, 1988), p. 111.
9. Indeed, Curley's translation of Spinoza's *Ethics* construes 2p10s2 in the following way: "But I have said that what necessarily constitutes the essence of a thing is that which, if it is given, the thing is posited, and if it is taken away, the thing is taken away, i.e., the *essence* is what the thing can neither be nor be conceived without, and vice versa, what can neither be nor be conceived without the thing." Samuel Shirley, on the other hand, construes this passage as: "But I did say that that necessarily constitutes the essence of a thing which, when posited, posits the thing, and by the annulling of which the thing is annulled; i.e., *that* without which the thing can neither be nor be conceived, and vice versa, that which can neither be nor be conceived without the thing" (my emphasis).
10. For Curley the collection of attributes is also identical with God.
11. However, Curley does translate 2p10s2 as: "*the* essence is what the thing can neither be nor be conceived without, and vice versa" (my emphasis).
12. My emphasis.
13. This may not be the case if *the* essence in 2p10s2 really means *an* essence for Curley. If this is the case, then "to constitute" the essence of would just mean "is identical with" *an* essence of a thing.
14. "What he [Spinoza] defines in Part II is not the expression 'essence', but the expression 'belonging to' (*pertinere*) as it applies to an essence": Donagan, *Spinoza*, p. 59. See also Alan Donagan, "Essence and the Distinction of Attributes", in *Spinoza: A Collection of Critical Essays*, ed. Marjorie Grene (Notre Dame, Ind.: University of Notre Dame Press, 1973), p. 180.
15. Donagan, "Essence and the Distinction of Attributes", p. 181. Donagan claims that the same argument can be made regarding the conception of God. However, if we replace "given" with "conceived" in Donagan's argument we get the following: "*Extensio* being conceived, an absolutely infinite being is also conceived; for *extensio* expresses an eternal and infinite essence, and whatever expresses such an essence is an attribute of an absolutely infinite being. Again, if, *per impossibile*, *extensio* were not conceived, there could not be conceived an absolutely infinite being; for, since *extensio* would not be conceived, there could not be conceived an absolutely infinite being." This argument does not go through—in the case where the attribute of extension is not conceived it does not follow that God is not conceived, because God may be conceived via any other attribute (e.g. the attribute of thought).
16. Donagan, *Spinoza*, p. 88.

17. Given the difference in the meaning of the terms "constitutes", "pertains to", and "is identical with" the essence of a thing relative to single-attribute and multi-attribute substances, it is difficult to know how Donagan understands these terms relative to the essence of a mode.
18. H. F. Hallett, *Benedict De Spinoza: The Elements of His Philosophy* (London: Athlone Press, 1957), p. 16.
19. Ibid., pp. 16, 20.
20. It seems that this would be the case unless Hallett were to claim that, while each particular attribute "constitutes" the essence of God, only the aggregate of indiscerptible attributes "pertains to" the essence of God. There is no particular reason to think that Hallett would hold such a view, since he thinks that in God there is no distinction of attributes.
21. Parchment, "The God/Attribute Distinction in Spinoza's Metaphysics", p. 61.
22. Ibid., p. 69 n. 24: "I take 'pertain to the essence' and 'constitute the essence' to be synonymous."
23. Ibid., p. 62.
24. Donagan, *Spinoza*, p. 89. Donagan does not give any particular reason for holding this view, nor does he cite any textual evidence that Spinoza uses the terms "constitute" and "express" in this manner.
25. Unless Bennett holds a different view regarding the essence of a mode. Indeed, this follows for each of the commentators. It would be inconsistent to hold one view on the relation between 2d2 and God and a different view on the relation between 2d2 and modes. So I will assume that for each commentator, whatever is the case for God relative to 2d2 must also be the case for modes relative to 2d2.
26. Spinoza clearly denies that God is a divisible entity. See 1p12 and 1p13.
27. Della Rocca agrees; see Michael Della Rocca, *Representation and the Mind–Body Problem in Spinoza* (New York: Oxford University Press, 1996), p. 95 and n. 26: "By '*actual* essence' Spinoza means the essence of an existing or actual thing. ... The term 'actual essence' is to be contrasted with 'ideal essence', which is the essence of a thing whether it exists or not."
28. Although in 3p6 Spinoza speaks of "things", the demonstration indicates that this proposition is limited to "singular things". Since God is not a singular thing, there is a certain liberty (justifiable, I think) in extending this conclusion to God. Also, Spinoza seems to deny that God literally *strives* to do anything; God is beyond striving. I take account of the special case of God in the next paragraph.
29. Baruch Spinoza, *The Ethics and Selected Letters*, ed. Seymour Feldman, trans. Samuel Shirley (Indianapolis: Hackett Publishing Company, 1982), p. 31.
30. See 1d6e. The NS includes the translator's interpolation, "we can conceive infinite attributes which do not pertain to its nature". It seems unlikely that this is a claim by Spinoza that we can actually conceive attributes other than thought and extension. Rather, it must be the claim that we can verbally

affirm that if something is infinite in its own kind then other attributes that do not belong to the nature of that substance nevertheless exist (i.e. it is the claim that we can conceive *that* they exist).
31. Bennett holds this view: see *A Study of Spinoza's Ethics*, p. 76.
32. See n. 30 above.
33. See Letter 56: "Here it should also be observed that I do not claim to have complete knowledge of God, but that I do understand some of his attributes—not indeed all of them, or the greater part—and it is certain that my ignorance of very many attributes does not prevent me from having knowledge of some of them."
34. See 1d6e.
35. 1p30d: "A true idea must agree with its object (A6), i.e. (as is known through itself), what is contained objectively in the intellect must necessarily be in nature."
36. 2p32d: "For all ideas which are in God agree entirely with their objects (by P7C), and so (by 1A6) they are all true, q.e.d."
37. "Nature" in 1p30d cannot mean the existing physical world, since we can have true ideas of things that do not (and perhaps never will) exist in space and time. See 2p8.
38. 2p34: "Every idea that in us is absolute, or adequate and perfect, is true."
39. 1p8s2: "Hence, if someone were to say that he had a clear and distinct, i.e., true, idea of a substance . . .".
40. In 2p38c Spinoza indicates that an adequate conception is a clear and distinct conception: "For (by L2) all bodies agree in certain things, which (by P38) must be perceived adequately, *or* clearly and distinctly, by all."
41. For a fuller account of the relation between adequacy and internality in Spinoza, see Della Rocca, *Representation and the Mind–Body Problem in Spinoza*, pp. 53–59.
42. Ibid., p. 108.
43. Ibid., p. 107.
44. Ibid., pp. 40–41: "Thus the collection of all ideas constitutes an individual thinking thing. For Spinoza, as we have seen, the human mind is simply a subset of these ideas. Since Spinoza regards the human mind as itself a thinking thing (2def3), it follows that, for Spinoza, one thinking thing is contained in another: the human mind is contained within the infinite thinking thing. Since Spinoza calls this infinite thinking individual the infinite intellect *of God*, I will, for convenience, refer to the infinite thinking individual as God's mind."
45. I will discuss these ideas later in this section.
46. Ibid., p. 54. Della Rocca explains: "For Spinoza, a necessary and sufficient condition for the inadequacy of an idea in the human mind is that the idea is caused by ideas that are not part of the human mind."
47. Ibid., p. 54.
48. Ibid., p. 55.

49. 2p9: "The idea of a singular thing which actually exists has God for a cause not insofar as he is infinite, but insofar as he is considered to be affected by another idea of a singular thing which actually exists; and of this [idea] God is also the cause, insofar as he is affected by another third [NS: idea], and so on, to infinity."
50. Della Rocca, *Representation and the Mind–Body Problem in Spinoza*, p. 56.
51. Della Rocca gives an example of a confused or inadequate idea in a human mind: "When, for example, I perceive the sun, I am really confusing a state of my body with (a state of) the sun. I am thinking of both my body and the sun in such a way that I do not, and perhaps cannot, clearly distinguish them. Spinoza's position is that any idea that is caused from outside my mind is confused in just this way. The idea is, confusedly, of a state of my body and of the external body that caused that state": ibid., p. 63.
52. See 1d4 and 1d6.
53. 3d2: "I say that we act when something happens, in us or outside us, of which we are the adequate cause, i.e., (by D1), when something in us or outside us follows from our nature, which can be clearly and distinctly understood through it alone. On the other hand, I say that we are acted on when something happens in us, or something follows from our nature, of which we are only a partial cause."

Chapter 7: The Essence of Spinoza's God

1. I will use the terms "idea" and "conception" interchangeably.
2. That is, if any given attribute pertains to the essence of God then when the attribute of thought is conceived, God is conceived, and when the attribute of thought is not conceived, God is not conceived. However, when the attribute of thought is not conceived it does not follow that God is not conceived, since God may be conceived through the attribute of extension.
3. See Chapter 4 n. 72. Also, if there is an infinite number of attributes, then the human intellect would be unable to have an idea of that which pertains to the essence of God (i.e. the infinite collection of attributes), since the human intellect can conceive only the attributes of thought and extension.
4. Donagan holds a similar view, since for him each attribute expresses the essence of God only in its kind.
5. For Parchment that which pertains to the essence of God is conceptually distinct from the essence of God; and it is unclear whether Parchment holds the view that any X and Y that are conceptually distinct are also strictly identical.
6. See Chapter 5 above.
7. "The thesis of parallelism simply states that there is a structural similarity between two separate explanatory or causal chains": Michael Della Rocca, *Representation and the Mind–Body Problem in Spinoza* (New York: Oxford University Press, 1996), p. 20.

8. Ibid., p. 19.
9. "An object has, for example, the property of being physical only relative to a certain manner of conceiving or describing it": ibid., p. 139.
10. Ibid., pp. 157, 167.
11. See ibid., p. 167: "On my interpretation of Spinoza, each attribute is a distinct way in which the essence of God (under a particular description or conception) is constituted."
12. "See 2def2. Actually, what Spinoza says is that a thing cannot be conceived without that which constitutes its essence. For Spinoza, to say that x cannot be conceived without y is tantamount to saying that x is conceived through y": ibid., p. 205 n. 20.
13. See 1d4 and 1d6.
14. 2p45: "Each idea of each body, or of each singular thing which actually exists, necessarily involves the eternal and infinite essence of God."

    2p46: "The knowledge of God's eternal and infinite essence which each idea involves is adequate and perfect."

    2p47: "The human Mind has an adequate knowledge of God's eternal and infinite essence."
15. See 2d2, and also 2p10s2: "The essence is what the thing can neither be nor be conceived without, and vice versa, what can neither be nor be conceived without the thing."
16. See Della Rocca, *Representation and the Mind–Body Problem in Spinoza*, p. 164: "So, it follows from Bennett's view that even if, for some reason, the individual who perceives thought and extension as constituting God's essence is not thereby in error, that perception does not give the individual a true and adequate idea of the essence of God."
17. See 1p10.
18. One might think that this argument will not go through if there are only two attributes. In this case the human intellect will have an adequate idea of the collection, i.e. the attributes of thought and extension. However, Spinoza claims in 2p1s that we can conceive an infinite being (God) through only one attribute. This conflicts with the view of God and God's essence as the collection of attributes. It seems that on this view the de re idea of God would be the idea of the collection of attributes (since the collection of attributes is identical with God).
19. See Michael Jubien, *Contemporary Metaphysics* (Malden, Mass.: Blackwell Publishers, 1997), p. 69: "Most philosophers do not believe that *de re* beliefs automatically follow from *de dicto* beliefs. The reason is that we often do have *de dicto* beliefs in cases where we have no significant contact with the person or thing that the *de re* belief would be about, so that the needed three-place relation linking us, the entity, and the property cannot take hold." The same conclusion can be drawn about de dicto and de re conceptions.
20. The totality is the entity wherein the attributes exist indiscretely.

21. See 1p10s.
22. Even if there are only two attributes, the interpretation of the essence of God as the collection of attributes is not viable since, according to 2p1s, the conception of more than one attribute is not necessary for the conception of God. Hence, the essence of God cannot be the collection of attributes, regardless of their number.
23. Della Rocca, *Representation and the Mind–Body Problem in Spinoza*, p. 167.
24. 3p4d: "For the definition of any thing affirms, and does not deny, the thing's essence, *or* it posits the thing's essence, and does not take it away."
25. Della Rocca, *Representation and the Mind–Body Problem in Spinoza*, pp. 165–68.
26. Ibid., p. 165.
27. There seems to be some similarity here between Curley and Della Rocca, since they both hold the view that God has many individual essences and one overall essence. For Curley each attribute is *an* essence of God while the collection of distinct attributes is *the* essence of God, while for Della Rocca each attribute is a way the essence of God (or the first-order essences of God) can be conceived or described, and all the attributes together is God conceived or described as the substance of infinitely many attributes (or the second-order essence of God).
28. Ibid., p. 167.
29. See Chapter 6, p. 75, "The relationship between a thing and its essence".
30. If the essence of a thing were just the thing (i.e. including all accidental and necessary qualities) then the term "the essence of the thing" would just be another term for "the thing itself".
31. See Jonathan Bennett, *A Study of Spinoza's Ethics* (Indianapolis: Hackett Publishing Company, 1984), p. 61. Bennett agrees that to say that the essence of X is X is to render 2d2 vacuous.
32. See Chapter 6, p. 77, "The relationship between a thing's essence and its power".
33. 1p34: "God's power is his essence itself."
34. 3p7d: "From the given essence of each thing some things necessarily follow (by 1P36), and things are able [to produce] nothing but what follows necessarily from their determinate nature (by 1p29)."

    1p16: "From the necessity of the divine nature there must follow infinitely many things in infinitely many modes (i.e., everything which can fall under an infinite intellect)."
35. Indeed, if something were expressed under one attribute and not another then the attributes would not express the same essence. Since there is only one substance—and each attribute expresses the essence of that substance—the attributes are necessarily parallel.
36. God's essence is expressed in other ways if there are other attributes. Gilles Deleuze also holds the view that the attributes express the essence of God. See Gilles Deleuze, *Expressionism in Philosophy: Spinoza* (New York: Zone Books, 1992), pp. 41–44.

37. See 1p16.
38. Baruch Spinoza, *The Letters*, trans. Samuel Shirley (Indianapolis: Hackett Publishing Company, 1995), p. 208, my emphasis.
39. 3p4d.
40. 1p8s2.
41. 1d6 Exp.: "I say absolutely infinite, not infinite in its own kind; for if something is only infinite in its own kind, we can deny infinite attributes of it [NS: (i.e., we can conceive infinite attributes which do not pertain to its nature)]; but if something is absolutely infinite, whatever expresses essence and involves no negation pertains to its essence."
42. 1a4: "The knowledge of an effect depends on, and involves, the knowledge of its cause."

    1p28: "Every singular thing, or any thing which is finite and has a determinate existence, can neither exist nor be determined to produce an effect unless it is determined to exist and produce an effect by another cause, which is also finite and has a determinate existence; and again, this cause also can neither exist nor be determined to produce an effect unless it is determined to exist and produce an effect by another, which is also finite and has a determinate existence, and so on, to infinity."
43. Della Rocca, *Representation and the Mind–Body Problem in Spinoza*, pp. 88–89.
44. Edwin Curley, *Spinoza's Metaphysics* (Cambridge, Mass.: Harvard University Press, 1969), p. 112.
45. For a discussion of Spinoza's position on "the essence requirement on representation", see Della Rocca, *Representation and the Mind–Body Problem in Spinoza*, pp. 84–106.
46. See 2p45–47. In the demonstration of 2p46 Spinoza says "that which gives knowledge of the eternal and infinite essence of God is common to all things, and equally in the part and in the whole"; and that this knowledge is adequate (by 2p38). The attributes are common to all things, and equally in the part and in the whole, since everything follows from the attributes.
47. Power unexpressed is no power at all.
48. This necessarily is the case given Spinoza's doctrine of parallelism.

Select Bibliography

Bennett, Jonathan, *A Study of Spinoza's Ethics* (Indianapolis: Hackett Publishing Company, 1984).

Curley, Edwin, *Behind the Geometrical Method* (Princeton, NJ: Princeton University Press, 1988).

Curley, Edwin, *Spinoza's Metaphysics* (Cambridge, Mass.: Harvard University Press, 1969).

Curley, Edwin (ed. and trans.), *The Collected Works of Spinoza*, vol. 1 (Princeton, NJ: Princeton University Press, 1985).

Della Rocca, Michael, *Representation and the Mind–Body Problem in Spinoza* (New York: Oxford University Press, 1996).

Descartes, René, *The Philosophical Writings of Descartes*, vol. 1, trans. John Cottingham, Robert Stoothoff, and Dugald Murdoch (New York: Cambridge University Press, 1985).

Donagan, Alan, "Essence and the Distinction of Attributes", in *Spinoza: A Collection of Critical Essays*, ed. Marjorie Grene (Notre Dame, Ind.: University of Notre Dame Press, 1973).

Donagan, Alan, *Spinoza* (Chicago: University of Chicago Press, 1988).

Hallett, H. F., *Benedict De Spinoza: The Elements of His Philosophy* (London: Athlone Press, 1957).

Jubien, Michael, *Contemporary Metaphysics* (Malden, Mass.: Blackwell Publishers, 1997).

Loux, Michael J., *Metaphysics* (London: Routledge, 1998).

Parchment, Steven, "The God/Attribute Distinction in Spinoza's Metaphysics: A Defense of Causal Objectivism", *History of Philosophy Quarterly* 13 (1996), 55–72.

Spinoza, Baruch, *The Ethics and Selected Letters*, ed. Seymour Feldman, trans. Samuel Shirley (Indianapolis: Hackett Publishing Company, 1982).

Spinoza, Baruch, *The Letters*, trans. Samuel Shirley, introd. Steven Barbone, Lee Rice, and Jacob Adler (Indianapolis: Hackett Publishing Company, 1995).

Index

adequacy, see idea(s)
adequate and inadequate 2, 62, 133
affections 4, 18, 39, 75, 122
attributes
  collection of 2, 4, 7, 9, 10, 13, 16, 19, 20–24, 27–30, 32–34, 41, 55–62, 66, 72–77, 88–90, 93, 96, 99, 101–102, 104–109, 118, 122–123
  discrete 4, 122
  distinct 20–22, 24, 28, 30, 37, 38, 41–42, 53, 55, 59, 74–77, 87–88, 92, 100, 105–106, 122–124
  number of 6, 11, 25, 28, 37, 59–60, 71, 78–81, 86, 89, 93, 114, 134
  relation of God to the attributes 1, 4, 14, 29, 91, 105–106, 120
  thought and extension 6, 22–23, 26–27, 52, 59, 60, 75, 86, 89, 100–102, 110, 112, 114, 116, 118, 132
  totality of 2, 4, 7, 9–10, 16, 19, 21, 37–38, 41–53, 59, 60–62, 68–69, 73–76, 84, 87–88, 92–93, 96, 97, 100–102, 106, 119, 126, 128, 130, 135

Bennett, Jonathan 2, 11–18, 28, 54–55, 62, 65–67, 72–74, 92, 96, 100–101, 121–122, 124
bundle theory 12, 20

causation 23
conatus 109
conception 2, 3, 8–10, 12, 14, 17, 18, 20, 21, 24, 27, 30–31, 37–38, 41–43, 46–51, 58, 63–64, 71, 74–75, 86, 87, 90–95, 98, 100–102, 104, 106–110, 113–115, 117–118, 120, 123–125, 128, 131
Curley, Edwin 2, 19–26, 28, 41, 55, 57–58, 62, 66–67, 71, 72, 92, 96, 113, 120, 122–123, 129, 131, 136

de dicto conception 2, 62, 86, 90, 93, 100–102, 135
de re conception 2, 3, 62, 86–87, 90–91, 93, 100–102, 104–105, 118, 135
definition 113
Deleuze, Gilles 136
Della Rocca, Michael 3, 18, 83–85, 91, 97, 98–99, 103–106, 108, 113, 122, 124, 128, 132–137
Descartes, René 42, 46, 127–128
  distinctio modalis 42
  distinctio rationis 42–44, 129
  distinctio realis 42
divisibility 28, 41, 55–58, 76–77, 88, 105–106, 126, 132
Donagan, Alan 2, 8, 28–33, 55, 57–58, 62, 67–69, 72–73, 92, 96, 124, 129–132, 134

essence
  and conatus 109
  and conception 2–3, 8, 12, 17–18, 20–21, 24, 27, 30–31, 37–38, 46–50, 63–64, 71, 74–75, 86–87, 90–95, 98–102, 104, 106–110, 113–118, 120, 123–125, 128, 131, 133–136
  definition of that which belongs to 56
  idea of 3, 9, 17, 21–24, 27, 38, 40, 46–49, 51, 54–55, 58–63, 71–72, 75, 81, 86–93, 96, 100–105, 107, 113–114, 116, 121, 129, 135
  of a thing 2–3, 6–9, 16–17, 21, 25–26, 30–31, 49–50, 62–78, 87–89, 93–98, 100–107, 112, 115, 117, 124, 130–132, 136
  of God 1, 3, 5–9, 13–18, 20–33, 37–80, 86–137
  pertains to the 8, 16, 31, 42, 49–52, 58, 60, 63–71, 79–80, 87, 92–99, 103–107, 110, 128, 134
  power and 2, 3, 8, 20, 35–36, 44, 62, 77–78, 81, 89, 91, 93, 107–120, 125, 136–137
eternity 78, 80
Ethics 1, 120, 121–124, 130–133, 136

Index of Passages Cited
  1a4 23, 37, 112, 123, 137
  1a6 28, 38, 40, 81
  1d4 5, 8, 14, 21–26, 28, 33, 39–41, 70, 103–104, 108, 123, 126, 129–131, 134–135
  1d6 3, 6, 8, 24, 26, 67, 70, 78–80, 89, 93, 103–104, 112–115, 117–118, 120, 129, 134–137
  1d6e 70, 79–80, 112, 132–133
  1p3 37
  1p4d 4–5, 19, 39, 122, 129
  1p8s2 82, 133, 137
  1p9 6

1p10 9–10, 22, 37–38, 80, 122–123, 126–127, 135
1p10s 55, 57, 59, 66, 76, 80–81, 123, 126–128, 130–131, 136
1p12 28, 55–56, 76, 132
1p12d 129
1p13 28, 56, 76, 126, 132
1p14 10, 24, 26, 121, 129
1p15 23, 123
1p15d 5
1p16 35, 136–137
1p16d 108
1p19 19
1p19d 69–70
1p20c 19
1p28 137
1p28d 18, 75
1p30d 81, 133
1p34 3, 8, 77, 91, 93, 107, 114–115, 118, 120, 136
2d2 2–3, 7–9, 14, 16–17, 21, 30–31, 49–52, 60, 62–68, 70–74, 87–88, 91–100, 103–104, 106–107, 109, 113, 117–120, 124, 128, 130, 132, 135–136
2d4 82
2p1 6, 9, 24
2p1s 9, 24–25, 53, 75, 117, 123, 129, 135–136
2p2 6
2p7 24, 83, 123, 129
2p7c 83
2p7s 13, 121, 128
2p8 133
2p9 85, 134
2p10 71
2p10s2 67, 70–71, 113, 131, 135
2p11c 84
2p29s 82, 85
2p32 28, 38, 126
2p32d 28, 81, 133
2p34 40, 81, 126, 133
2p38 23, 137

2p38c 133
2p43d 82
2p45 22–23, 61, 87, 128, 130, 135
2p46 23, 40, 61, 87, 128, 130, 135, 137
2p46d 23, 123
2p47 9, 22–24, 40, 55, 61, 87, 128–130, 135
3d2 35, 125, 134
3p4d 136–137
3p7 115
3p7d 77–78, 136

existence 6, 7, 12, 14–16, 35, 39, 42, 56, 63, 64, 66, 71–72, 74, 78, 87–89, 92, 94–95, 111, 137

God
  attributes of 1, 3, 6, 8, 19, 29, 39–40, 89, 92, 97, 98, 103
  conception of 2–3, 9–10, 14, 17, 18, 20, 21, 27, 30, 37–38, 43, 46–49, 58, 64, 87, 91–95, 98, 100–102, 106–108, 114, 117, 120, 123, 131, 136
  definition of 113
  essence of 1, 3, 5–9, 13–18, 20–33, 37–80, 86–137
  existence of 64, 78, 87, 92
  mind of 83–84, 86, 133
  nature of 42, 79–80
  power of 78, 81, 111, 116
Grene, Marjorie 124, 131, 138

Hallett, H. F. 2–3, 35–40, 47, 59, 62, 68, 73, 75, 92, 97, 125–126, 128–129, 132, 138

idea(s) 3, 9–10, 12–13, 17, 21–24, 27–29, 38, 40, 43, 46–49, 51, 54–55, 58, 60–61, 63, 71–72, 75, 81–93, 96, 100–105, 107, 110, 113–118, 121, 123–124, 126, 129–130, 133–135

adequate and inadequate 2–3, 9, 17, 21–24, 27, 38, 40, 43, 46, 48–51, 54–55, 58, 60–63, 72, 75, 81–85, 87, 89–91, 93, 96, 100–102, 104–107, 110, 113–116, 124, 129, 134–135
clear and distinct 82–83, 85, 89
confused 82, 134
of non-existent objects 81, 83, 86
true and false 9, 28–29, 38, 40, 81–86, 89, 92, 121, 133
individuals 31, 124
infinite 2–3, 6, 8–9, 18–28, 31, 35–37, 41–42, 44, 47, 51, 56–57, 59–60, 62, 67, 71, 78–81, 83–84, 86, 89–90, 93, 96, 98–99, 103–121, 123, 125–126, 128–137
  eternal and 1, 3, 8–9, 22–23, 26, 31, 35–37, 67, 78–81, 89, 93, 107–112, 114–118, 120, 123, 131, 135, 137
intellect 9–10, 14, 16–18, 21–24, 27, 30, 36, 38, 40, 46–47, 51, 54–55, 58–60, 72, 75, 83–89, 93, 96, 100–102, 104, 107–111, 114–115, 118, 129–130, 134–135

Jubien, Michael 135, 138

knowledge 9, 23, 31, 54, 60, 82, 100, 112, 118, 123, 133, 135, 137

Letters, The
  Letter 9 15, 19, 129
  Letter 36 110
  Letter 56 133
  Letter 60 81
  Letter 64 121
Loux, Michael J. 122, 138

mind
  God's 83–84, 86, 133

mind (*cont.*)
  human 22–23, 35, 61, 63, 81–87, 89, 93, 109, 113–114, 116, 118, 133–134
  modes 1–2, 5, 11, 13–19, 35–36, 40, 51, 54, 62, 66, 72–76, 88–89, 96–98, 100–101, 103, 109, 118, 121–122, 132, 136
  trans-attribute 13–18, 54, 73–75, 88, 96, 101–102, 121

Nature 80, 133

objective 6, 12, 15, 39
objectivism 39–41, 120

parallelism 24, 83, 86, 97, 108–109, 129, 134, 136–137
Parchment, Steven 2, 3, 40–52, 60–62, 68–69, 73, 75, 92, 97, 120, 125–130, 132, 134
perception 58, 126, 135
perfection 1, 42, 111
properties 2, 11–12, 15–18, 31, 36, 54, 62, 66, 72–74, 82, 100, 122, 124

reason (*ratio*) 7, 18, 43–45, 48, 66, 69, 89, 105–106, 127, 131–132, 135

Shirley, Samuel 121, 123, 131–132, 137
Spinoza, Baruch 1–8, 11, 13–15, 19, 21, 25, 33, 35, 38, 39–41, 55, 59, 62, 64–66, 69, 72, 74–76, 79, 80, 83–84, 88, 91–93, 97, 99–100, 103, 111–118, 120–138
subjective 6, 12, 15, 39, 55, 59
subjectivism 5, 12, 39, 41
substance 4–5, 8–9, 11–12, 14–15, 19–21, 24–26, 28–30, 32–33, 39–41, 56–57, 66, 68–70, 73, 75, 79–80, 97–99, 103–104, 106, 108–109, 112, 114, 115, 117, 120–124, 126–129, 131, 133, 136
  nature of 56–57

theory of reality 1
trans-attribute differentiae 13–18, 54, 73–75, 88, 96, 101–102, 121
truth, *see* ideas, true and false 2, 14, 16–17, 62, 73–74, 83